Leon Brown, backstage, Brooklyn Academy of Music

REVISED AND UPDATED

Pumping Iron
The Art and Sport of Bodybuilding

Written by Charles Gaines

Photographs by George Butler

Designed by Martin Stephen Moskof

Creators Publishing   Hermosa Beach, CA

Publisher's Note

Pumping Iron was first published in 1974 and updated in 1981 to include women's bodybuilding. The following is a reproduction of the 1981 edition but with the original 1974 cover, and it includes a foreword by Arnold Schwarzenegger and a new introduction by Charles Gaines. They offer their reflections on the changes in bodybuilding and fitness—and this book's impact on our world—over the past half-century.

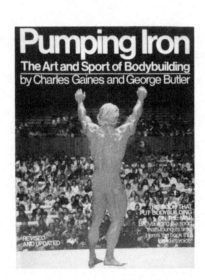

Also by Charles Gaines and George Butler
Staying Hard

Also by Charles Gaines
Stay Hungry
Dangler

Also by George Butler (with David Thome)
The New Soldier

The authors gratefully acknowledge permission to reprint lines from "The Leg," from *Selected Poems* by Karl Shapiro, copyright 1944 by Karl Shapiro, published by Random House, Inc.; and thank Mr. Joseph Weider of *Muscle Builder Power* magazine, 21100 Erwin Street, Woodland Hills, California, for permission to use material from the magazine.

Fenwick, by Mai Hancock, reprinted by permission of Chronicle Features.

Published by Creators Publishing
Creators Syndicate Building
737 3rd St
Hermosa Beach, CA 90254
310-337-7003

Designed by Martin Stephen Moskof
Manufactured in the United States of America

1 2 3 4 5 6 7 8 9 10

Library of Congress Cataloging in Publication Data
Gaines, Charles, date.
    Pumping iron.
    1. Bodybuilding—History. I. Butler, George,
date. II. Title.
GV546.5.G34 1981   646.7'5   81-16527
                                        AACR2

ISBN (print): 978-1-949673-89-0
ISBN (ebook): 978-1-949673-76-0

Arnold Schwarzenegger, Sydney Harbor, 1980

This book is dedicated to the people and sport it describes, and particularly to Joe Disco, Arnold Schwarzenegger, and Franco Columbu.

Foreword

Fifty years ago, the book *Pumping Iron* changed the world.

In the 1960s, when I arrived in America, no one knew what a bodybuilder was, so they would say to me, "You're big! Are you a wrestler? A football player?" For the people who did know about it, the image of bodybuilding was so terrible that the famous action movie stars of the time refused to admit they'd ever touched a weight. The few gyms that existed were dungeons or tiny studios with homemade equipment that most reasonable people avoided at all costs.

I've never been reasonable.

I have always been a crazy dreamer, and as my bodybuilding career took off and I collected enough Mr. Universe and Mr. Olympia trophies, I had a bigger vision. I wanted to start a bodybuilding and fitness crusade, to inspire everyone to see the benefits of weight resistance training, instead of thinking weightlifting was for Olympians and freaks. I studied to be a salesman as an apprentice in Austria and learned the value of marketing, and I then wanted to sell the sport of bodybuilding. I told people that one day, there would be more gyms than supermarkets in America, and they all thought I was crazy.

But then I met Charles Gaines and George Butler, who were in the middle of writing a book called *Pumping Iron*. They wanted to get a view from the inside of the sport, so I spent a few weeks hanging out with them. They saw something in me and in bodybuilding, and I saw something in them: amazing talent that could help this sport reach the masses. It was a perfect relationship. With George's unbelievable photography, Charles's crisp and beautiful writing, and my big personality and joy of promotion, bodybuilding was finally ready for its time in the spotlight.

The rest, as they say, is history. The book was released; artists from Andy Warhol to Jamie Wyeth to LeRoy Neiman wanted to paint bodybuilders like me; the press wanted to talk about lifting weights; bodybuilders were posing as an art exhibit at the Whitney Museum with serious artists and critics; and the message finally reached the people. The book was such a huge hit that we got back together for the movie, *Pumping Iron*, and soon, we were at the Cannes Film Festival and I was on every late show.

Pumping Iron launched my career. But more importantly, we cemented the bodybuilding and fitness crusade as completely mainstream. The fact that the book in your hands is still being reprinted after fifty years—a feat almost unheard of in the publishing world—tells you all you need to know about the impact it has had and continues to have. It has been printed in more than a dozen countries and sold well over one million copies in its various editions.

I tell people over and over that I am not a self-made man. That's because of people like Charles and George. I did not create this crusade alone. I needed them, I needed the press, and I needed the people.

Today, there are gyms in every hotel, hospital, military base, YMCA, sports club, fire station, police station, high school, college, and shopping center in the world. Every actor details their training regimen when their next action movie hits theaters. People become famous just for lifting weights on Instagram and TikTok.

And, by the way, today there are more than 106,000 gyms in the United States. There are 63,000 supermarkets.

We did it.

Keep reading, and keep pumping,

Arnold

Arnold Schwarzenegger, 2022

Introduction
to the 2022 Edition

The book *Pumping Iron* was first published in the winter of 1974, when nobody in the world but my buddy Johnny Gunn and I knew what the term "pumping iron" meant, and before anyone outside the small world of bodybuilding had ever heard of the man who would become the #1 movie celebrity in the world and governor of California.

In the introduction to that book, I wrote that its photographer, George Butler, and I thought of it as "a sort of respectful report from the interior of an interesting, colorful, and heretofore ignored region of American life," and that what we had tried to do in the book was "to chart, with some accuracy and a proper sense of wonder, the heart of (that) terrain."

The map of the terrain that was published in 1974 was an accurate one, and as good as we could make it. But it was not one George and I believed many people outside of the bodybuilding world would be interested in, and we were more surprised than anyone when, shortly after the book's publication, it reached and clung to a spot on the *New York Times* bestseller list. What we should have known was that the Mount Everest we had discovered and described in our two years of explorations in research for the book would be as fascinating and inspiring to many, many people outside of bodybuilding as he was to us.

Arnold Schwarzenegger was our Mount Everest, both in the book and the feature documentary that was made of it. Almost single-handedly he brought bodybuilding out of the shadows it had languished in since its earliest days in America and into the limelight. And if the book and the movie helped him to do that, he helped the book and movie far more. Arnold *legitimized* the sport and art of bodybuilding and gave it both dignity and a sense of humor—two attributes it sorely needed. Even if he had not won seven Mr. Olympia titles, he would be remembered for that reason alone as the greatest bodybuilder of all time.

The fact that the original book *Pumping Iron* did as well as it did was, as I have said, largely due to Arnold. But the fact that it ever came to exist was entirely due to two men who must be mentioned here: Bob Dattila, my volatile and irrepressible agent at the time, who was the first person outside of George and myself to believe in the book; and Dan Green, then an editor at Simon & Schuster, who, after we had been turned down by three publishers, took a chance on what I'm sure seemed to that urbane gentleman of arch tastes as icky a subject for a book as pedophilia. Shit happens. And so does luck once in a while. I do not have a doubt that without Dan and Bob, the phenomenon of *Pumping Iron* never would have occurred.

It was to investigate that phenomenon and do an update on bodybuilding for a revised edition of the book that Dan and Simon & Schuster sent George and me back on the road in the late '70s. In the introduction to that revised edition, published in 1981, I noted that what we discovered was that though much had changed in the terrain of bodybuilding, much remained the same. The dominant forces in the sport in 1971–Arnold, Franco Columbu, Frank Zane, Mike Katz, Ken Waller—were still around and winning pretty much any competition they went into. But there were new stars, too, among them Mike Mentzer, Tom Platz, Boyer Coe, Dennis Tinerino, Chris Dickerson, and Jusup Wilkosz. Bodies, contests, and prize money were all larger for both the men and the women. But the most significant change, we found, was that bodybuilding itself had "arrived" in America, come out of its closet and taken a seat in the living room; and we also found that the major thing that bodybuilding in 1981 had in common with itself in 1974 was that the man who had put it in the living room was still the king.

****

It is now almost half a century since the book *Pumping Iron* left the station and over forty years since the revised edition was published. I have not kept up much or regularly with what has happened in bodybuilding since 1981. I do know that there have been other kings and queens in the sport since then, such as Ronnie Coleman, Dorian Yates, Lee Haney, and "Big Ramy" Elssbiay in the men's division; and Bev

Francis, Carla Dunlap, Corinna Everson, Lenda Murray, Iris Kyle, and Andrea Shaw in the women's. I know, too, that the bodies in both divisions have gotten far bigger and more ripped, in some cases to a truly mind-boggling extent: Any one of the finalists for the 2021 Ms. Olympia title, for example, could have easily won the 1981 *Mr.* America contest. Whether or not this is an altogether good development is a matter of taste; but it does seem worth mentioning my perception that the bigger and more "unreal" the men's and women's musculatures have become, the more distant they appear to the general public's taste in archetypes for the perfection of male and female bodies.

Which may mean that the train of bodybuilding's popularity outside its own world—a train that left the station back in 1974 with the original publication of this book—might be close to reaching its terminal. Or already there. Or nowhere near there. Arnold Schwarzeneggers are rare as hen's teeth, but that is not to say that another one won't come along and carry bodybuilding into another golden age.

I know I speak for my great friend and ideal collaborator George Butler, who left us in 2021, in saying that he and I were privileged and grateful for witnessing and reporting on the first golden age. And George's son, Desmond Butler, and I are also most grateful to Rick Newcombe and his Creators Publishing for making this reprint available to a new readership.

Charles Gaines
Seafields, Nova Scotia

July 2022

Introduction
to the 1981 Edition

Before the original publication of this book in the winter of 1974, the phrase "pumping iron" belonged to a number of people I could count on one hand—a raggedy bunch of bodybuilders including myself who hung around the Magic City Health Club in Birmingham, Alabama, in the late 1950s. Now, in 1980, the phrase appears to belong to the whole country. I don't go a month without reading or hearing it somewhere—in a *New Yorker* or *Esquire* cartoon, in a somber essay on narcissism in the *New York Times Sunday Magazine*, from the silly mouth of a TV sports commentator—and whenever I do it makes me smile. It makes me smile every time I hear or read the words "pumping iron" because it makes me think of my man, Johnny Gunn, who was the first person I ever heard use them and who, so far as I know, invented them.

We were sixteen, Johnny Gunn and I. The context would be like this.

"Where you going, Gunn?"

"To pump arn in Fred Crabbe's basement."

Pump *arn*—TV commentator, *New Yorker* cartoonist and all the rest of you—was the *right*, the *original* way to say it. Gunn wasn't a hick; he could have said it the way the rest of you do now if he had wanted to, but he liked his way better. So did I, and I still do.

Back in the late 50s and early 60s when Gunn and I pumped arn together, with Fred Crabbe in Crabbe's basement and then at the Magic City Health Club, we could have referred to what we were doing with some phrase of Swahili and it wouldn't have mattered to anybody. The fact was that outside of a tiny number of people, and most of them in California, nobody in the country knew anything about bodybuilding or wanted to. That was still true in 1972 when the photographer George Butler and I first began to do magazine articles on the subject, and the fact that it was made us suspect that there might be a good book on the subject. There was. There was also a good movie, titled with the same bastardized version of Johnny Gunn's phrase. And at the center of both the book and the movie was a natural force, you might say—an undiscovered star for whom stardom was only, ever, a matter of time, and a big enough one so that once he was discovered a lot of people were forced to notice for the first time the thing that he did. Most people become stars because of their *métier*, a few in spite of it. Arnold Schwarzenegger is one of the few: America discovered bodybuilding because it happened to lie next to Arnold Schwarzenegger.

In the original introduction to this book I wrote that sometimes during the traveling we did as research for *Pumping Iron* George and I felt a little like nineteenth-century explorers, poking around in a subject as primeval and unmapped as parts of Labrador. That feeling was unambiguous and thrilling. Recently we have felt more like the old guy up the road from me here in New Hampshire who sold to developers two hundred acres of woodlands that had been in his family since before the Civil War, and moved to Florida on the profits. Not long ago he was back up in New Hampshire visiting and he went out and stood on a bluff and looked down at the houses and yards, the paved roads and garbage cans and garages now occupying his old family land. Well...sure he liked Florida. Sure he was well off now and didn't have to shovel snow or cut wood, but..."I tell you, Charles," he said after a while, "you just shoulda *seen* them woods in the fall."

Pumping iron has been taken up all right—not just the phrase but the preoccupation—in a way none of us back at the Magic City Health Club would have bet a Joe's chili dog could happen. And since the original publication of this book the terrain of bodybuilding has been as radically altered as my New Hampshire neighbor's land. There are roads out there now, towns and fast-food joints. Viewing it from a bluff, so to speak, in 1979, Butler and I didn't know whether we liked the looks of the place or not anymore. We did know for sure that we no longer knew our way around, and if we felt a little of my neighbor's nostalgia, we also felt, every time we came back to the bluff, more and more curiosity. What was it like out there now? Who were the new people who had moved in, and how had the old ones changed? In 1980 we said to hell with it, and just trucked on down off the bluff to find out. We started going to contests again; we met a lot of new people and checked up on all the major characters in the original book. This new edition of *Pumping Iron* carries, along with new photographs, a written report on all that—a two-part report, one on the terrain and one on the state of the art and sport.

It carries as well a message to Johnny Gunn: Hey Gunn, they may know all about it now, but they still can't say it right.

FENWICK   by Mal Hancock

© CHRCANGLE FEATURES 1972

"FRANKLY, FENWICK, I GET MORE PERSONAL SATISFACTION FROM 'PUMPING IRON' THAN ANYTHING ELSE IN LIFE!"

Introduction

I have been involved with bodybuilding in one way or another since I was sixteen years old. I began lifting weights then and have done it lazily and noncompetitively ever since. I have also written about it previously in a different form. This book grew out of that involvement and, specifically, out of a story for *Sports Illustrated* that George Butler and I did in the summer of 1972 on the Mr. East Coast contest which was held in Holyoke, Massachusetts, and won in that year by Leon Brown. Since then we have been to quite a few places tracking bodybuilders, seeing contests and putting together the materials here. If we felt at times a little like 19th-century explorers, it was because we found bodybuilding to be as primeval and unmapped as parts of Labrador. Nobody, we discovered, had been back into it to send out a report on what it was like.

This struck us then as peculiar, and it still does. America is a country of subcultures, and most of them, including ones as esoteric as midget wrestling, pimping and the Roller Derby, have been thoroughly explored and documented. Like those activities, bodybuilding is an obsession, a living (for a few), and a way of life for the people involved in it—a subculture, in a word, with its own values, aesthetics and vocabulary. The fact that it seems to us a far more fascinating and resonant one than any of those other three might sound simply practical for the authors of a book about it, but it is also true. And yet no one had undertaken seriously to describe it. To our knowledge, this is the first book ever on the subject.

Young Arnold

In the Middle East bodybuilding is the second most popular spectator sport. There, and in Japan, Australia, the West Indies, South Africa and parts of Europe, its competitions are national events. There are probably a number of reasons why it has never taken hold like that in America, and one of them certainly is that almost since its beginnings here, bodybuilding has advertised itself with consummate tackiness, confining itself to the back pages of pulp magazines and, in the national consciousness, to the same shadowy corners occupied by dildos and raincoat exhibitionists. Unflattering myths developed early here. And the composite picture that seems to have emerged from them, of bodybuilders as narcissistic, coordinatively helpless muscleheads with suspect sexual preferences, has done little to promote the sport.

Part of what we have tried to do is to demonstrate that this is an inaccurate picture. We have also wanted to describe truly something of the sport, art and life of bodybuilding, and to suggest in passing that if you have never been to a good physique contest you have definitely missed something.

But mostly we think of this book as a sort of respectful report from the interior of an interesting, colorful and heretofore ignored region of American life. It does not attempt to be comprehensive, and to anyone who finds himself—or something he knows or represents—skimped or omitted, the authors apologize. What it does attempt to do is to chart, with some accuracy and a proper sense of wonder, the heart of the terrain.

We want to thank Patricia Gaines and Brooke Hayward for their grace and high sense of fun during the process of putting this book together. A lot of other people have been helpful. We are grateful to all of them and would like to acknowledge these especially: Dr. Larry Golding, Ben and Joe Weider, Sig Klein, Enrico Natali, Tom Minichiello, Dietz Heins, Jeri Wentz, Charles Roman, Tom Kinney, Wayne and Karen DeMilia, Joe Gold and the Honorable Zabo, Paul Graham, George Synder, Frank Zane, Ed Corney, Leonard Olsen, the Ferrigno family, and John Herman.

Charles Gaines
George Butler

Pumping Iron

Part One
The Training

"The body, what is it, Father, but a sign
To love the force that grows us, to give back
What in Thy palm is senselessness and mud?"

—Karl Shapiro

"For soule is forme, and doth the bodie make."

—Edmund Spenser

One
Mr. Olympia No. 1

At 10:45 the house lights go down and the Brooklyn Academy of Music falls seriously quiet for the first time all evening. Martin Stader, master of ceremonies and former Mr. Universe, says the following:

"Ladies and Gentlemen, the first contestant in the 1973 Mr. Olympia contest. From France . . . Serge Nu*bret*."

The old-fashioned music-hall curtain is raised, and there, spotlighted on the posing dais in profile to the audience, as underdressed as his introduction, is the massive and fabled Nubian Lion. It is his first appearance in America. The aficionado crowd is reticent at first, busily checking him over as it would a touted European car—part by part, kicking his tires, squinting up at those famous pectorals as though they might have a French accent.

Nubret waits for a moment for the noise level to rise, and then begins with a set of swooping side shots, putting his best up in front of the judges right away—the tiny waist, vacuumed into a comma, the unusually high and well-formed pectorals that slope from his collarbones like hogback ridges, the cantaloupe-sized deltoids. And the arms. Nubret's arms, it is clear, are as dangerous as they are reputed to be: massive, symmetrical, the muscles cleanly divided and balanced. No disappointment there, and the crowd tentatively begins to hype. He does the single bicep pose with his right arm, keeping his left behind him, fist cocked at the hip in a tricep flex . . . holds it . . . and pivots to face the judges to begin his front shots.

But, with the turn, something mysteriously escapes Nubret's routine; vitality seeps fatally from it like gas from a soufflé.

Serge Nubret

Arnold Schwarzenegger
Mr. Europe, AAU Mr. World, 5
times Mr. Universe, 4 times and
current Mr. Olympia.
26 years old
6'2" tall
240 lbs.
57" chest
22" arms
31" waist
28" thighs
20" calves

At the squat rack, Gold's Gym

Wrist Curls

Franco Columbu
Mr. Italy, Mr. Europe, 3 times
IFBB Mr. Universe, 3 times IFBB
Mr. World
30 years old
5'5" tall
185 lbs.
50" chest
19" arms
30" waist'26" thighs
17 ½" calves

Franco Columbu

He has swung into position for most of the favored bodybuilding poses: the double-biceps, the most muscular. It is an instant when he should have the crowd rising to him, the applause and whistles and moans shaping into proper tumult. But something happens, and Nubret's promise, his sense of potential, his mystery, is gone. Bodybuilders call it disappearing. The celebrated weaknesses, his back and legs, suddenly seem to leap into neon. The crowd continues to applaud, but he has lost it. It has gone subtly and irrevocably polite on him.

The rest of his routine is as lackluster as heavy machinery being moved around. He goes through his front and back poses seriously and awkwardly, stumbling occasionally on the dais. One notices a bodybuilder's face at such times, and Nubret's handsome West Indian features remain so composed, so removed from the situation, that his expression begins to seem part of the problem. It's as thoroughly joyless and preoccupied as an astronaut's. It is also resigned. He knows he has just kissed off one year's worth of training.

That's how long Serge Nubret has savaged himself for this year's Mr. Olympia contest—ever since the same competition last September in Essen, Germany, where he placed third. And a year is big money to Nubret. In addition to being Mr. France and one of the preeminent bodybuilders in the world, he is a movie and television star in France and the owner of a chain of Parisian gyms. World-class bodybuilding takes more time than a businessman-actor has to give, and, win or lose, this is his last contest. But he wanted this one badly. It is the biggest title in bodybuilding—one for which only the four or five best professional builders in the world can compete—and he wanted it for Guadeloupe, an island that he left twenty-three years ago for France and where he is now an almost completed legend.

For the last twelve months, for three hours each morning, three each afternoon and two each night, Nubret has pushed and pulled maniacally at iron while sustaining a diet that would explode an ordinary metabolism—doing for that renowned chest, for instance, forty sets of twenty benchpresses (pushing 210 pounds off his chest a total of eight hundred times every other day) and ingesting nine pounds of meat, four hundred grams of protein supplement and thirty-two glasses of water *daily*.

It is a slightly crazed schedule. And to support it, it is not hard to imagine Nubret developing, in the late recesses of one of his gyms, where all thought of money and movie fame is banished for a year, the mirthless purpose, the grim sense of do or die, that he brought with him to New York.

Nine AM, two weeks before the contest in New York: a chest, back and leg day at Gold's Gym in Venice Beach, California. Outside, a fog curls down Pacific Avenue, blanking the windows and isolating

"Chuck Sipes was strong but I am much stronger than him. Very much stronger than him. All around. Because he was strong on the benchpress. I'm strong in everything. Any kind of movement you can find in a gym, I can beat everybody in it."

—Franco Columbu

Check posing

"When I was ten years old I got this thing that I wanted to be the best in something, so I started swimming. I won championships, but I felt I couldn't be the best. I tried it in skiing, but there I felt I didn't have the potential. I played soccer, but I didn't like that too well because there I didn't get the credit alone if I did something special. I just avoided team sports from then on. Then I started weight lifting through the other sports and I enjoyed it the most. I won the Austrian championship in 1964 but I found out I was too tall. So I quit that and went into bodybuilding. Two years later I found out that that's it—that's what I can be the best in."
—Arnold Schwarzenegger

Pullovers

Benchpresses

the gym—making its peculiar energy seem singular and lonely as an atom's.

Inside, Nubret's competition, the other two contestants for the Mr. Olympia title, are beginning a morning of their own type of training. Outsized diagrams of railroad cars join in a frieze about the mirrored wall. Beneath them Arnold Schwarzenegger, "the Austrian Oak," is happily pushing 315 pounds twelve times off his supine self. Smooth, flat-back repetitions: the black Olympic bar falls to his chest, pauses, rises, three 45-pound plates, big as manhole covers, jiggling at either end. Schwarzenegger is the current Mr. Olympia. He also happens to be the best bodybuilder alive, and very possibly the most perfectly developed man in the history of the world. He came to this country in 1968 from Graz, Austria, brought over by an American muscle entrepreneur named Joe Weider. When Weider found him, Schwarzenegger had been a competitive swimmer, soccer player, skier, boxer, wrestler, shot-putter and javelin thrower; he had been the weight-lifting champion of Austria and the curling champion of Europe; he was Mr. Europe and Mr. Universe—and he was all of twenty-one years old. Now, at twenty-six, he has won five Mr. Universe titles and the last three Olympias, and he has not lost a contest since 1969. It is a record of total domination in bodybuilding that compares with Pele's in soccer, or Merckx's in cycling, or Killy's in skiing. That kind of outrageous superiority is always subject to demeaning imputations. And there are people around who will tell you that Schwarzenegger injects himself with silicone, or that he uses truckloads of anabolic steroids. The truth is simply that he was born with more physical talent, is smarter at the sport, and works at it with more joy and fierceness than any other bodybuilder in history. That, and one other thing: he has wanted to be the best at something, the very best, since he was ten years old.

As always there is a knot of people watching him. Three of them, Kent Kuehn from Florida, Denny Gable from Iowa, and I, will follow the set, using progressively lighter weight but sweating more and breathing harder. Kuehn calls it chasing Arnold. This is the fourth set of benchpresses. There will be five more; then there will be five sets of presses on an inclined bench, five sets of dumbbell flyes and two sets of twenty cable flyes—all designed to bulk, shape, striate and clarify the pectoralis muscles of the chest by means of a fearful tearing down of tissue there. At this early moment in the routine I, for one, could testify truly that the tearing down occurs. But as you watch Arnold's fifty-seven-inch chest, which resembles an ordinary man's the way a Waterford punch bowl does a fruit jar, spreading and humping ornately under the weight, you are aware of the ache in your own as someone playing tennis with Rod Laver might be aware of blisters. Pain is growth around here. The men in this room, many of them, have come from all over the country just to be able to hurt with Arnold.

Between sets

There is a quality of festiveness, a strong sense of celebration, at Gold's that you don't find at other gyms. It has to do with pride. Many of the biggest names in bodybuilding are regulars—Franco Columbu, Frank Zane, Dave Draper, Ken Waller. And hotshots from all over the world make annual pilgrimages here. More than half the winners of the three big September contests in New York will come from this one gym, and the people here know it. They know Gold's is where it's at. And they know why. It is mostly because of the six-foot-two-inch, 235-pound Austrian over there doing benchpresses. He attracts the best because he states their case. They come from all over to follow his training, and also because he is the embodied articulation of what they do. The people standing around now watching his chest are looking at *an idea made fact*—a chest carried out of mind to absolute and final form. And there is another thing. Because he is a natural, cleaving as closely to this strange sport-art as a piece of Saran Wrap to a table, to watch him train is to glimpse immediately and vividly what is most real about the development of a body for exhibition. Other bodybuilders can read the true grain of their commitment through him as easily as they can count the divisions of muscle beneath the skin on his chest.

Finished with the set, he stands up, tugging at his shorts. and surveys the gym, his gray eyes prowling for anything new that might have developed. Over by the chinning bar, dressed in a red tank suit and high-topped shoes, doing bent-over rows with three hundred pounds, is his best buddy and the third Mr. Olympia contestant—a massive and puckish Sardinian named Franco Columbu, who looks as if he ought to smoke thin cigars in Italian Westerns. At five feet five inches and 185 pounds, he is one of the strongest men alive for his size, and the only bodybuilder other than Arnold to make his living at it. The two of them travel together all over the world on exhibition tours, but they don't have much to do with each other here in the gym. Arnold yells something to him in German. Franco leers briefly and answers. Both men have an ability to make their slightest gestures seem important, and the whole gym taps into this exchange. These are the two Head Men, each riding his own momentum into the last two weeks of an eight-month blitz for the same title; God knows what they might be saying. But Arnold doesn't continue the conversation. He makes a little circle around the gym, clapping a shoulder here, gibing somebody there—pulling things together. Then he ambles back over to the bench, lies down, and grabs off the new weight like a haunch of turkey.

As the morning progresses there is much laughter, sweating and spillage: messy, boisterous, intent—the weights clanging like tableware—the activity comes to resemble a medieval feast. On the floor the shanks of barbells gleam like bones. The other dozen or so men in the gym struggle and rest to separate rhythms, yet they are all connected to the same central energy: to the digestion of exercise, the turning of work into themselves. It is a visible process and a riveting one—much more than vanity, it is the reason why a bodybuilder studies himself in mirrors. Watching a muscle after working it, he can see the freshly oxygenated blood flooding the tissue, spreading and flushing the skin, creating the condition known as a pump—the sacramental engorgement of muscle that is an outward and visible sign of growth. A pump is the fix and rush of bodybuilding. It produces a feeling that is wonderfully clearheaded, self-sufficient and refreshed—as though all the blood were new. The feeling spills over and fills the gym. The fog at the windows that covers all of Venice Beach might as well have eaten it; and with it, all those people out there who don't know a Mr. Olympia from a Mr. Des Moines. Gold's Gym is buzzed on a pump. Together. Doing fine.

Two

First there are the big-city gyms—places like Tom Minichiello's Mid-City in Manhattan and Julie Levine's R & J in Brooklyn, which are two of the best. A few very good bodybuilders like Leon Brown and many others who are not so good have come out of these places. But there is usually a depressing sense of anonymity about them, and a lot of the people there do not look happy while they are working out. A few of them look overtly hostile, as if the energy of the workout were tickling them with violence. Some look unpleasantly lost in themselves. Some just look sad. But practically no one looks happy. You wonder about people who don't look happy while they are working out, because very few things feel better to the body. Whatever the reason, it is only in these big-city gyms that you find many of them.

Then there are the "spas," the fancy health clubs like the ones owned by Jack La Lanne, or like the old Vic Tanney chain, which got very big in the fifties and then went broke. The spas feature individualized training programs, carpeting, pretty chrome weights and a lot of unnecessary reducing machines. They try hard to cater to business and professional types, and they usually don't encourage serious bodybuilding, though a few will play both ends of the street by stacking some black weight off in a room by itself for anyone redneck enough to want to use it. They all glitter, these places. The attendants are usually bulky, smiling people dressed in white uniforms. Very few good bodybuilders come out of "spas."

Almost every YMCA in America has a weight room, and most of the ones I know about are wonderful places to train.

Robbie Robinson

Lou Ferrigno, R and J Studio

"They say we are muscle-bound and freaks. Well, I tell you the truth, man: I never really pay too much attention to these people. The more they talk, that's the more I'm going to continue working out. Because that's the way I feel about it. It's the thing I want to do and I'm going to continue. I don't care what they say. . . . I think that it's a very good thing and I'm going to continue with it as long as the Lord leaves me breath and I have the strength to go along with it. I'm going to be doing it all the time."
—Lawrence Samuel

They always have good basic equipment, and you know while you are working out that you can go upstairs afterward and smooth off with a run or some basketball. Y gyms are generally good-humored places. Some of the funniest talk I've ever heard came out of a Y gym I used to go to in Atlanta. At the one I use now there is a stocky, javelin-throwing former Mr. New Hampshire powerlifter named Punky Stewart. Punky Stewart wears red-white-and-blue shoes and a bright-red halter when he works out. He walks in dressed like that, chewing gum very fast, and eyes the Olympic bars lying around like a dog looking at table scraps. Then Punky will start grinning. He grins right through every exercise and everything he says, and when he goes upstairs to shower he is still grinning.

Mike Katz used to use a Y gym in Hartford, Connecticut. Mike is a funny guy and it is easy to imagine that that gym was a very good-humored place. But after he won the IFBB Mr. America contest in 1971, people at the gym started to heavy up with him, so Mike began working out in a garage with just his training partner, Joe Ugolik, and Coach, a nice old guy who helped train Mike and who owned the garage.

George Butler and I were there at Coach's garage one day when Mike and Ugolik were working legs. It was early spring and still cold, so the first thing they did was to fire up an 85,000-BTU torpedo-shaped space heater. The heater made a constant whooshing noise and put out a hard, old-fashioned smell that suited the place. The garage was full of old weights and machines that Coach had made, all of them functional, and arranged precisely around the walls so that there was good space in the middle. Mike and Ugolik began doing leg presses, working from 310 up to 650 pounds in six sets—lying on their backs under the weight, legs spread wide above their chests, letting their thighs come all the way down to their armpits before they pushed up the platform. And Coach stood in the middle of the slowly warming garage watching them use the equipment he had made; and helping by talking up the weight.

"Nice and easy," he told them over and over, rubbing his hands together. "Push it way up. Atta*boy*, Mike. *Way* up, now"—watching them the way you might watch someone you cared about riding a horse you had trained.

The very best places to do bodybuilding, though, are the few gyms run just for bodybuilding by someone who doesn't care particularly about overweight businessmen. These places, like the very best bars, never make all the money they could make, and sometimes they don't make any money at all, which probably accounts for why there are so few of them. I have been in only two of these places. One is gone now. It was in Birmingham, Alabama. Gold's Gym is the other one, and it is doing fine out in Venice. The guy who owns Gold's, I understand, doesn't need the money. The guy who owned the one in Birmingham went broke and moved to Florida. They say Vince Gironda's Gym in North Hollywood is in this category, and George Eifferman's in Las Vegas, and Bob's Gym in Fremont. I don't know; I've never been to those places. Tom Minichiello's place in New York would be if it weren't for all the unhappy-looking people, and they are not Tommy's fault.

What these places have in common, besides less income than they'd make if they were "spas," are these things: good equipment, good people, good humor and the right feel. The feel of a really good bodybuilding gym has to do with a sense of inevitability of what's done there. If the feel is right, it causes you to believe while you are there that there is nothing in life so worthwhile or fun or exciting as pumping iron.

One person, if he's big enough, can give a place this feel.

The place in Birmingham was called the Magic City Health Club. It was on the second floor of a brick building right in the middle of town. Between sets you could look down through the big picture windows at what was happening out on Second Avenue, and the hurry out there always made you feel glad that you were up where you were with no place to go. In the summer somebody would open the fire-escape door in the back, and the wonderful mustard-and-meat smell from Pete's Hot-Dog Stand would drift through the gym, speeding up the workouts as it started to work on people. There were a lot of big boys using Magic City in those days who stayed hungry and who could flat-handle a hot dog. Eating six or seven after a workout and before dinner just to kick back at that smell was not unusual.

Billy Joe Barrett, two or three times Mr. Birmingham and almost a Mr. Alabama, used Magic City then. And Pee Wee Suits, who might have done something except for his calves. And Richard "Radar" Coe, who could have won just about anything around but came from the Country Club side of the mountain and so couldn't compete. It was a good group and a funny group, but it was Joe Disco who gave the place its feel.

Disco came from Ohio. Maybe. He was twenty-eight or thirty-four. He might have had a master's degree, and been married at one time, and had a lot of money. Nobody really knew, because Disco was creative with his past. It was a part of his art to tinker with it. Of his present, you knew that off and on he managed the health club; that sometimes, when he had money, he drove a sports car and lived in a swank apartment building with a swimming pool; and that other times, when he didn't, he stayed in a rooming house in Five Points and lived off coffee and protein pills. He trained, but not for competition anymore. He might have been a Mr. Universe. He claimed to have invented a revolutionary bowling glove and a system for

"I would spend an hour a day, maybe a year in advance of a contest, just on posing. I used to pose to music all the time. I would work at it just like a dance step. The music was a part of my routine; the lighting was a part of it. It was just like being on the Ed Sullivan show—it was an act. I had an act and I stuck with this act like a professional artist. Everywhere I went I had my own lighting, my own staging, my own platform, everything."
—Bill Pearl

Bill Pearl at his club in Pasadena

Coach, Mike Katz and Joe Ugolik, West Hartford, Conn

renting towels to high school gyms, either one of which could make him rich overnight, but he didn't let them out because he didn't want the hassle.

Joe didn't want to get hung on anything outside the gym. The gym was his pivotal place; one half of him was stuck there, like the pointed arm of a compass, and he wanted that other arm free to move. He loved the gym. He relished the work and fun and pump of working out and what it did for you and how it made you feel, and he made everybody else relish it, too—made them feel that nothing else was nearly as important.

That summer and fall of my wife's first pregnancy, just before we left the South, she and I and Joe would walk in the evenings down to Joy Young's Chinese Restaurant for dinner after working out. Joe had her working out, too, downstairs in the ladies' section. The three of us would swing out of Magic City through the warm cottony Alabama dark with Joe talking and with Patricia in the middle, leaning a little to aft, and laughing her fine deep laugh. Heading for egg rolls and sweet-and-sour pork, feeling sinfully clean and brand new and very fresh and clear in the head, we felt on those walks as if we owned the sidewalks. That's the way a really good gym will always make you feel.

Aside from a flashy red, white and blue sign over the door, Gold's Gym is not a very interesting-looking place from the outside. It's a chunky one-story buff-colored building, hunkering so close to Pacific Avenue that three steps out the door puts you into the middle of traffic. But inside it's exactly right. In the back there is a small office and a protein bar. Above them are showers and a locker room. All the rest is gym.

It is a bright, pleasant, uncrowded room with a high ceiling, big enough for fifteen or twenty men to work out at the same time without getting in each other's way. To work out with, there are two or three tons of weight lying around. Dozens of black iron dumbbells are racked in pairs along two walls, ranging in size from 5 pounds up to around 150. There are also barbells whose weights are fixed at various poundages up to a hundred pounds or so, and for anything heavier than that there are three or four Olympic sets.

An Olympic barbell is the basic piece of bodybuilding equipment, as central to it as an iron is to golf. The bar is seven feet long and weighs 45 pounds with the collars. The best ones are made of cadmium steel. Its central section is about the same diameter as a garden hose, and the knurled gripping lengths come into the hands as comfortably as the handle of an old ax. At either end of the bar there is a two-foot section, twice as big in diameter as the shank, onto which the black flanged cast-iron plates are slid. You can get six 45-pound plates on each end of an Olympic

bar without the collars. That would bring its weight to 585 pounds, and not a lot of people need any more than that. There are a few at Gold's who do. For them there are one-hundred-pound plates.

There are also machines: custom made, many-stationed unit gyms like the Universals; lat machines; leg-press, hack-squat, leg-extension and cable-flye machines. There are even a couple of the relatively new Nautilus machines, chrome-and-Naugahyde contraptions that look like sophisticated torture devices. These are very chic machines right now. They are made by a man in Florida who claims they are revolutionizing bodybuilding. They are rarely used at Gold's. Most of the time they just sit there without the dignity of people in them, looking lonely and menacing.

If you happened to wander into Gold's off the street, and if you had never been in a bodybuilding gym before, it would seem as confusing as the inside of a clock—the oddly shaped metal everywhere, the cables and counterpoised masses of the machines, the mysterious-looking inclined benches and squat racks and sit-up tables. Right, you would tell yourself; but what is all this stuff supposed to do? If you had an uncommon eye for metaphor, you could maybe get an idea by looking up at the huge, intricate diagrams of railroad cars above the two long walls of mirrors. It is the simple function of those confusing pictures to clarify the internal structure of large things. So it is with the sprawl of equipment here. On any given morning during the summer you would find a group of very big men using that equipment loudly to clarify their bodies for competition.

Training is what they call it, and the way they do it here is so arresting that even if you were a person who does not care very much about bodies or about the people who do, if you had any kind of eye at all you would probably decide to hang around until it was over.

An old guy I knew in Iowa used to say that the only two parts of himself that interested him were his hands and one other part, and that his hands were only good for getting that other part out of his britches. Bodybuilders are less basic. They divide themselves up into six areas, or muscle groups: the back, the shoulders, the chest, the arms, the legs and the stomach. For a builder to do anything in competition, no one of these areas can be significantly less developed than the others, so a good bit of attention goes into balancing the training of all. The training of a muscle consists of first tearing it down with concentrated exercise, then allowing it to rest so that the tissue grows back a little larger than it was before. Because it is necessary for a muscle to rest while it grows and because of the importance of balanced development, most competitive bodybuilders train on a split routine: they

Denny Gable, Gold's Gym

43

I Front
1. Deltoid
2. Pectoralis Major
3. Biceps
4. Serratus Magnus
5. Rectus Abdominis
6. External Obliques
7. Rectus Femoris
8. Vastus Externus
9. Vastus Internus

II *Back*
1. *Trapezius*
2. *Triceps*
3. *Latissimus Dorsi*
4. *Biceps Femoris*
5. *Gastrocnemius*

1

2

3

4

5

Ken Waller doing dumbbell benchpresses

Donkey calf-raises

work certain parts of the body one day and rest those muscles the next while they work the others, alternating like that six days a week.

There are many different ways to split a schedule. Ed Corney, for instance, who trains up in Fremont, likes to work his stomach, shoulders and back together and to do an hour and a half of his workout in the morning and the other hour and a half in the afternoon. Here at Gold's, on Monday, Wednesday and Friday they train the chest, the back and the calves in the morning, and the upper legs and the stomach in the afternoons. On Tuesday, Thursday and Saturday they do shoulders, arms and calves in the morning and use the afternoons for tanning.

This is a Monday morning, around 9 a.m. A few people like Dave Draper who train early have already showered and gone. Franco Columbu, who starts at eight and likes to work out alone, is already into his lats. In the back there are four or five guys joking around, warming up while they talk. None of them lives here in California. Kent Kuehn and Denny Gable are from the South and Midwest. Bill Grant and Russell Long are from cities back East. And Pierre Vandensteen is from Belgium. Like the others he is here because this is training season, because this is Gold's, and because of the Austrian who is just now parking his silver BMW Bavaria in the lot outside.

Ken Waller stands behind the protein bar with a towel around his neck, thumbing a magazine. Before Waller got into bodybuilding he played pro football in the Canadian League; now he manages Gold's. He has red hair, freckles and a tough, country face. He is the only one who doesn't look up when Schwarzenegger swaggers in and throws a towel at the boys warming up in the back, a couple of whom have been waiting on him for fifteen minutes. "Come *on*, you guys," Arnold tells them. "I'm tired of waiting for you guys. Let's get *going*."

Where he and Gable and Kuehn go, as soon as Arnold changes, is across the room to a foot-and-a-half-by-five-foot Naugahyde-covered, metal-braced bench to begin work on their chests—on the pectoralis muscles, called pecs, that lie between the collarbones and the rib cage. More than the arms, more even than the back, the chest is the seat of upper body strength. It is the bear's muscle—whose main and converse functions are to push things away from the body and hug things to it—and when developed properly it is very beautiful: two clean downward sweeps from the windpipe to the armpits and then an open flaring into the shoulders that give the body ovalness and depth above the waist. For some reason, maybe because they lie so close to vital organs, or because of the warm, dense, quick pump they take, the pecs are probably the most satisfying part of the body to work. And the primary exercise used to work them, the benchpress, is one of the most satisfying of all exercises.

Schwarzenegger lies flat on the bench. At its head, behind his shoulders, are two pronged vertical arms that hold the Olympic bar a few feet above his face. Planting his feet wide on either side of the bench, he works his hands on the knurled bar for the place where it feels right, where it will ride evenly across the middle of his palms. Then he pops the bar off the prongs. As he lets the weight down he inhales to fill his lungs for pushing. The bar falls, touches his chest just above the nipples and rises, he exhaling with it, so smoothly that the motion looks pneumatic—seems to happen in a lubricated sleeve. Twelve times he lets the weight down and pushes it up, the pecs spreading to the fall and bunching to the rise like fists opening and closing. Each lift is called a repetition, or rep; twelve of them are a set. He and the other two men will do nine sets apiece, increasing the weight as they can for the first four and decreasing it as they must to get twelve reps for the last five. There is no waiting between sets, and no one is off the bench for more than a couple of minutes at a time.

This kind of competition training is known as bombing. It is a savage combination of the slow, heavyweight sets normally done to develop size and the quick high-rep work with lighter weights that develops definition and muscular clarity. In its energy and speed it is very exciting to watch, and murderous to do. Almost immediately the chest begins to hurt—a steady burning at first that turns into a deep raw ache of tissue and grows, so that the hardest sets are done through the most pain.

After the second or third set a rhythm develops. They are on and off the bench in smooth, quick rotation. The breathing is heavier and deeper. They talk the weight up for each other: "Keep it tight. . . . Push it now"—the mean-looking steel bar dropping and rising in a slight convex curve from the plates stacked at its ends. All of it—the sweating and concentration and noise—builds and synchs in around the central experience of the exercise: the flow of richly oxygenated blood to the muscle, the flush and tightening of skin as the tissue feeds and swells, coming up warm and heavy-feeling as though the work and pain, or even some of the iron itself, had been shoved in under the skin.

This is called a pump. It is the workout gone inside: the exercise swallowed and digested, metabolizing visibly into growth. Some bodybuilders will tell you that it feels better than coming. Whether that is true or not, it is one of the finest and most complicated physical sensations you can have. The part of the body being pumped feels like one of those fast-frame films of flowers blooming or seeds ripening; the muscles seem actually to go from pod to blossom in seconds under the skin.

A pump also makes you feel giddy and happy in the head, and as Schwarzenegger, Kuehn and Gable feel it coming up and watch it in the mirrors, they begin to grin like Punky Stewart. Between sets they poke at their chests and stretch them out to feel the pump as far down as it goes. There are at least a half-dozen people around who are also pumped by now, and a general intaking exuberance, pleasuring and rowdy as a good party, spreads through the gym.

There are two kinds of exercises in a bodybuilding routine: the ones that build mass, or bulk as builders call it, like benchpresses for the chest, or squats for the upper legs, or bent-over rows for the back; and the ones whose function is to clarify the bulk—to carve and shape it the way you whittle a block of wood. The magical notion at the heart of the sport is that the body itself is an art medium: malleable, capable of being aesthetically dominated and formed the way clay is by a potter. A bodybuilder in training is a kind of sculptor of himself—the parent of a design of his body which he puts into competition with other designs. The traditional way of practicing the art is to bulk up with heavy weights and all the food you can eat, gaining twenty or thirty pounds of fat and muscle beyond where you want to be for competition, and then in the last month to go on a protein diet and chisel away all the fat with high-speed clarifying exercises, leaving only muscle. Bodybuilders call the last part of this process razoring, or cutting up, or ripping. They are all accurate words. But most of the best modern bodybuilders don't bulk and cut like that anymore. They work out fast with heavy weight, keeping themselves close to the skin. They bomb all the time, combining in their routines some exercises for bulk and some for cuts, and they hardly ever have a lot of fat to lose.

Roger Callard demonstrates upper thighs

After the benchpresses, Schwarzenegger and his training partners do five sets of barbell presses on an inclined or slanted bench. This exercise concentrates and peaks the movement at the top of the chest and carves out the fine lateral striations on either side of the sternum. More than any of the other chest exercises, it hurts. They do five sets of twelve reps, hurting—Arnold more than the other two, because he does the exercise with greater purity. By the third set the enormous biceps that are his most incredible muscles—like two grapefruit on greased tracks inside his arms—have begun to quiver, and his upper chest is red and painful-looking as a cyst. One reason why Schwarzenegger is the best bodybuilder alive is that he never cheats an exercise. He makes every movement full and clean without jerking or pausing and without borrowing from muscles other than the one he is working. Another reason is that he concentrates so well.

Concentration in bodybuilding means thinking a muscle through what it is doing—forcing it with your mind, and with your eyes if you can stare at it, to work fully. As an ability, particularly in the definition exercises, it is one of the great sheep and goat

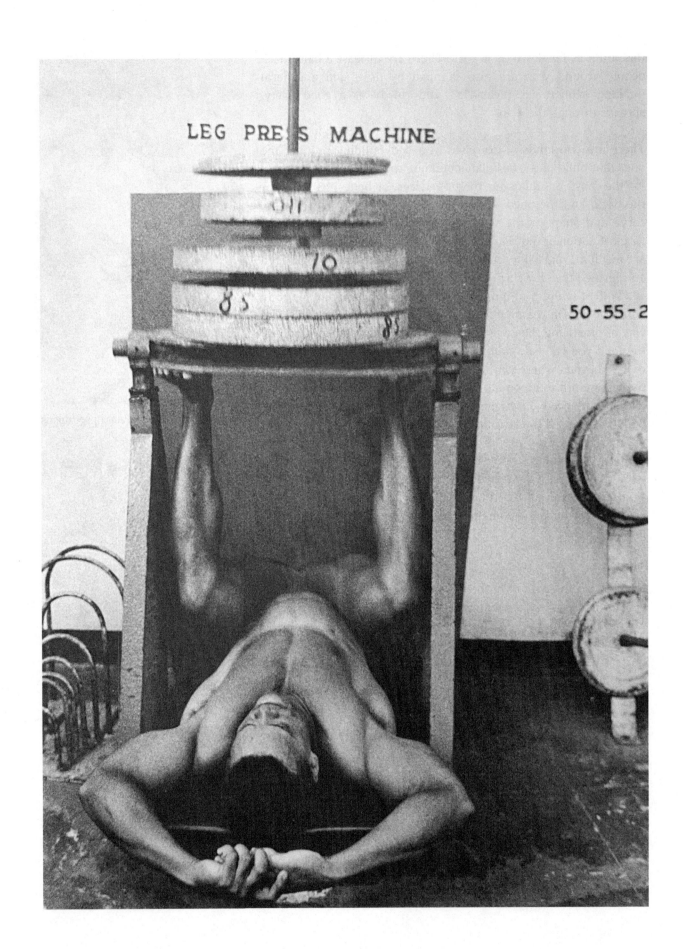

separators of the sport. The people who cannot manage it very well tend to stay smooth. And all the best bodybuilders can block out an air war with their concentration. I remember watching Ed Corney doing dumbbell curls in Baghdad. He was seated on a stool in the middle of the big, strange gym that the city let the Mr. Universe competitors work out in. There must have been thirty or forty Iraqis standing along all four walls, and another fifty or so at the windows looking in. Ed Corney sat in the middle of all those fervid, noisy little people, staring at the sheath of his bicep fill and empty, fill and empty, his face remote and rapt as a Yogi's, his mind somewhere down inside the fibers of that arm.

After the inclined presses come five sets of dumbbell flyes and, finally, two sets of cable flyes. Both these exercises are designed to work the outside curves of the pectorals and their tie-ins with the deltoid muscles of the shoulders. Dumbbell flyes are done lying on a flat bench. The two weights are held over the chest and brought slowly down and out away from the body until the elbows are below the plane of the bench and the pecs are stretched back and out as far as they will go. Then the arms are pulled back upward in a curve toward each other—"Like you are hugging your girl," Arnold puts it—but only three-fourths of the way up, so that tension is kept on the muscles. For cable flyes, you stand and pull the handles of two weighted, pulleyed cables from above the head and beyond the shoulders, down across the body to meet in front of the crotch.

When they have finished with these exercises, Schwarzenegger, Kuehn and Gable will have made their chest muscles push or pull against metal a total of 278 times. Then they will go to work on their backs.

Across the gym, Franco Columbu is just finishing up on his, looking very professional as he always does when he is working out. He moves around the room from set to set with the aplomb and economy of an operating surgeon. Like Schwarzenegger, Franco is a natural athlete. At various times he has been a race car driver, an equestrian, a soccer player, a powerlifter and an amateur boxing champion of Italy. He has great charm and physical presence, and a highly developed sense of himself. You do not have to be told that Franco is very good at what he does. As with Arnold, there is an unmistakable aristocratic sheen, a polish of quality, on everything about him. He believes he will win the Olympia contest this year, and with good reason. He is as muscular as his small frame will allow, yet symmetrical and delicately carved. Except for his height he might have beaten Arnold before. He believes he can beat him this year despite it.

To start his back routine he did six or seven sets of wide-grip, behind-the-neck chins, wearing a dumbbell on a strap around his hips to make them harder. Then rows, bending at the

Leg presses, Young's Health Studio, Montego Bay, Jamaica

waist so that his upper body was parallel to the floor, and pulling up a barbell fifteen times to touch his abdomen. And then more rows, this time with a bar that has one end fixed to the floor and the other weighted with plates, crouching over the weighted end and pulling it to his chest. (Franco can do twenty-five repetitions of this exercise with three hundred pounds on the bar—a fact that doesn't really impress until you try one with that weight.) For his last exercise he is seated, facing a cable machine with his feet braced in front of him. Slowly, with as much stretch as he can manage, he draws two handles, connected by cable and pulley to two hundred pounds, from his feet to his upper abdomen and lets them back again. The muscles doing the work fan out on either side of his rib cage like wings.

Latissimus dorsi: they are called lats. They originate from the lower six thoracic vertebrae, the lumbar and sacral vertebrae (by means of the lumbardorsal fascia) and the crest of the ilium, and attach at their widest points to the humerus bones of the arm. Their functions are to rotate the arms medially and to draw the shoulders downward and backward. What all that physiological talk doesn't tell you is that the lats are the muscles you would use to lift a tree off someone. Nor does it tell you what glamorous and cocky things they are. Seen from the front of the body they flare out behind the chest in a wide V from the waist line to the upper arms, giving width to the torso and a curved depth of field to the rounded, ornate muscles of the chest and stomach. From the rear they are thicker-looking, and hump out from the spine like two legs of mutton to form an elegantly simple base for the convoluted smaller muscles in the upper back and shoulders. When they are developed, and particularly when they are pumped, the lats hold the arms out a little from the body, forcing the elbows wider than the shoulders. This way of standing or walking is the most identifiable physical characteristic of bodybuilders. It is their trademark, like a wrestler's neck.

The trapezius, rhomboideus, infraspinatus, teres and levator scapulae are small, fancifully curved muscles lying near the lats that look in a good back pose as if they might have been shaped with different cookie cutters. When they are pumped, they bunch and tighten into a comfortable back-straightening countertension with the swell of the lats. And when that feeling is added to a chest pump, as it is in Franco right now, the whole upper torso feels dense and coiled and powerful as baled wire. It is a wonderful sensation, all that tightness—so satisfying and right that you are sure while you have it that it is the way a man's chest and back are supposed to feel all the time.

Franco does his last set of pulley rows feeling like that, enjoying them one at a time, stretching each one out to pull down deeply into the muscles. Two or three weeks from now on a stage

"Bodybuilding should be fun because you get a feeling of satisfaction which is very hard to explain. A bodybuilder knows that when he pumps up his muscles it means growth. The muscles grow. So therefore he knows when he pumps up well, that is progress. And that satisfies him because he feels the progress in his body. Therefore the pump feels good. It's actually the best feeling a bodybuilder can have."
—Arnold Schwarzenegger

Frank Zane check-posing

in New York he will want every line and cut he can bring up now, and knowing that makes the exercise even more enjoyable. Working out is always fun for him, but it is most fun in these last weeks before the contests when the training has to be flat out, and when everybody is around and into it together, creating a sense of shared momentum and priority. In the gym and on the beaches and in the health-food restaurants, there are people around now who haven't been around since this time last year —from New York, all over—everybody bombing and catching rays and razoring off: Franco and Arnold for the Olympia; Waller and Grant and Maldonado for the World; Kuehn, Birdsong, Jeff Smith, Leon and others for the Mr. America. For all of them this time of year out here is a rite, a festival of eating and tanning and training that is done together to finish themselves into contest shape. It is also a time of self-criticism and revision, when they demand and get the most from themselves. That is really what Franco likes most about it. This is his time of year.

Kent Kuehn is sitting on a bench watching Bill Grant stand up on his tiptoes and then drop back flatfooted—up down, up down, like that on a machine, pushing up around three hundred pounds each time on his shoulders. Kuehn, Gable and Arnold have finished their backs and are into the fourteen sets of calf raises they do to polish off a Monday morning.

"Come over here and get a picture of Grant's calves before they disappear," Kuehn tells George Butler. "You'd never know this man spent three years in a wheelchair. Hey, Bill . . . Bill," he says to Grant, who is grunting out his last five reps, "what I want to know is how in the hell those little suckers can burn that much."

Grant is not amused. He has worked the muscles in question until they felt like they were going to explode, and still they won't come up right for him. Finished with the set, he looks wistfully over to where the best calves in the business are now busy doing donkey raises—pushing up two men astride Arnold Schwarzenegger's vast, horizontal back. The inner and outer gastrocnemius muscles in each of Arnold's calves swell out and downward from the back of the knee, meeting in a cloven bulge like an upside-down heart. They are satyr calves: flamboyant, breathtakingly tooled shapes that up until a couple of years ago were his poorest muscles—a body part he consistently gave away in competitions against Sergio Oliva, the great black Cuban builder from Chicago, who was then, as he is now, Arnold's only real competition.

Arnold decided they had to be bigger, better-shaped and lower on his shins. He made them that way by lifting weight and people with them over fifteen hundred times a week. And, more crucially, by mentally forcing them to conform with what he

Curls

55

thought they ought to look like. Even for him the body is a reluctant medium. It resists final forms with a vengeance, and to snap that resistance, to develop a calf or any other part of the body into what it is capable of being, requires hundreds of hours of demanding more than it wants to give—of pushing not only against the inanimate weight but with the mind against the organic recalcitrance of tissue.

By eleven-thirty all the people who started training around nine are finished. The calf workout ends, and the morning is abruptly over and silent. If you have been watching, Gold's feels suddenly like an auditorium or theater when a long applause stops all at once.

Franco showers quickly and leaves for a steak, green vegetables, yogurt and wine at his chiropractor fiancée's house.

Arnold will crowd his girl friend and a party of guys from the gym into his BMW and drive to some place like the Brownbagger—where, wearing emerald-green shorts and a T-shirt, looking as fancy and outrageous as a unicorn, he will cruise ahead of everybody else across a patio of small people eating spinach salads, and through the crowded main room to his table, where he will order a side dish of four scrambled eggs with his Stuffed Sirloin Spectacular, and tell a snowed and gaping hippy waitress that he doesn't vont the bread because it's not on his special sex diet.

And this afternoon between four-thirty and six, after lunch and a couple of hours on the beach, he will be back here with Franco and Kuehn and Gable and the others to work his stomach and his upper legs—doing dozens of sets of squats, front squats, hack squats and extensions for the long ellipsoid muscles of the frontal thigh, and leg curls for the biceps femoris muscles that run from his butt to the rear of his knees.

But before he does all that, and before he showers, he walks over to one of the big mirrors and takes off his shirt. The gym goes even quieter than it was before, and everyone still in it stops whatever he is doing. Looking thoughtful, Arnold turns his right calf forward and flexes it, watching in the mirror as the cleft muscle leaps into complicated relief. He twists it; studies it. Then he does the same thing with his left calf. Then he jerks both arms straight out in front of him and flexes his chest, and the motion seems to throw a fine sharp spray of excitement around the room. The men standing behind him watch the mirror in the same elated, adrenalized way you watch a fight as Arnold checks himself through five or six quick poses, his face now grinning and appraising wolfishly. They are all bodybuilders, a few of them very good ones, and they have all seen Arnold pose before, yet they stare at the reflection like the ladies on Santa Monica Beach when they see a builder for the first time.

"You don't really see a muscle as a part of you, in a way. You see it as a thing. You look at it as a thing and you say well this thing has to be built a little longer, the bicep has to be longer; or the tricep has to be thicker here in the elbow area. And you look at it and it doesn't even seem to belong to you. Like a sculpture. Then after looking at it a sculptor goes in with this thing and works a little bit, and you do maybe then some extra forced reps to get this lower part out. You form it. Just like sculpture.
—Arnold Schwarzenegger

Dumbbell flyes

Arnold and his mother

"The better you get, the less you run around showing off as a muscle guy. You know, you wear regular shirts, loose shirts—not always trying to show what you have. You talk less about it. It's like you have a little BMW—you want to race hell out of this car, because you know it's just going 110. But if you see guys driving a Ferrari or a Lamborghini, they slide around at 60 on the freeway because they know if they press on that accelerator they are going to go 170. These things are the same in every field."
—Arnold Schwarzenegger

It's not just his size that does this to people. There are a number of bodybuilders around who are as big, and a couple who are bigger. More than that, it is the perfect balance of everything—of biceps to calves, shoulders to waist, thighs to chest—and the detail and clarity of every part. Another thing is the naturalness and grace of his body. Most of the other very big builders, like young Lou Ferrigno, who has the greatest size ever but no polish, yet, look as if they have been built up with a trowel: the muscles look stuffed and worried into place. But each of Arnold's body parts, though huge, is subtly refined—as sleek and graceful-looking as the hind leg of a thoroughbred racehorse.

This quality is known as finish. It is the ultimate achievement for a bodybuilder, and it is very difficult to get. Of the men in Gold's Gym now only Pierre Vandensteen, the little Belgian whose upper body looks carved out of ice, has it. But the rest can recognize it whenever it is put up in a mirror for them, and see in it what each of them is working toward—where, with luck, the sweat and pain and discipline of this morning and all the other training goes.

None of them moves until Schwarzenegger is finished check-posing the muscles he has worked. Nobody wants to. They all know they are somewhere special, doing something important. One person, if he is big enough, can give a place this feel.

Three
Mr. Universe No. 1

George Butler and I went up to see Mike Katz and Ed Corney around two o'clock on the afternoon of the Mr. Universe contest. They had a room together on the floor above ours in the Hotel Baghdad, and they were asleep in it, taking a nap between lunch and some last-minute sun on the hotel roof.

We woke them up. They were lying in the low twin beds that were more like raised pallets than beds, covered to the waists with striped wool blankets, and neither of them seemed very chipper. Because of the heat and the heavy food and all the strange sensations, it took everybody a long time to come awake in Iraq.

"What time is it?" Ed Corney wanted to know. When he heard it was two he groaned. "We got to get some sun," he told Katz. "Pop out of there, big fella."

Katz just lay on the little bed, his eyes blank and unfocused, as though he were listening to himself wake up. He was propped on a pillow at the headboard, the muscles of his upper body segmented and hard-seamed as the carapace of a lobster.

Despite the armor-plated look, and despite his enormous size and the fact that he was for four years an offensive guard for the New York Jets, Mike Katz is a vulnerable-looking man—particularly when he laughs, or when he has just been awakened. He has a solemn, angular face, the only part of him that looks undernourished. He believes it is an ugly face and that it has always held him back. But it isn't ugly—or vacant and mean, as it can seem at first. It is intelligent and, once you know what you are looking at, vulnerable, and a little awkward, like his movements. Mike learned how to hold his face and how to move

Ed Corney
1972-73 IFBB Mr. America, 1972-
73 IFBB Mr. Universe
40 years old
5' 6 ½ " tall
170 lbs
48" chest
19" arms
29" waist
26" thighs
17" calves

as a cross-eyed fat kid who was picked on in Hartford, Connecticut. Now he is the favorite for the title of Mr. Universe at the 1972 IFBB World Body Championships in Baghdad, Iraq; he is also a teacher and only a dissertation away from a Ph.D.—but he still does those things the same way.

At thirty-nine Ed Corney is eleven years older than Mike Katz, and he does not look even a bit vulnerable. He looks cheerful and self-possessed, and gentle in the way genuinely tough men usually do. About a year after the time in Baghdad I was at a party in a New York restaurant with Ed when an uptown lady began to needle him. She was sitting next to him and was a little drunk and maybe didn't know how to talk decently to him, so she began calling him "Mister" Corney, and began needling him about what he does for a living. What he does is bounce—thoroughly, and as nicely as it makes any sense to do that job—at a nightclub called Mr. Magooz in San Jose, California. Ed listened to her say she had never known a bouncer before and what a charming thing that was to do, and answered her when she asked him what he thought about when he bounced, smiling at her and calling her ma'am, but not in the same way she was calling him mister. He had paid out of his own pocket to come to New York for a contest he had not won. He was only two months off a big knee operation, and six off a second divorce. He needed her kind of talk like another bad knee, but he could see that this lady smoked and drank too much and, in her small, sharp face, that she was a lot worse off than he was.

He was born and raised in Hawaii, and his own face is broad, vaguely Asian, and very expressive, especially when he is posing. He got into bodybuilding late and has had good luck with it, but a lot of bad luck in other parts of his life. One of the pieces of good luck was that he learned how to pose from Clancey Ross, and nobody now poses with more joy, triumph and beauty than Ed Corney does. He doesn't have Katz's education, but he is bright, and very articulate about things that are important to him. He doesn't talk at all about the things that aren't.

At the time, he was the IFBB Mr. America. He had won the title two months before in New York, and winning this one in Baghdad too would give him the America and the Universe, two of the three biggest amateur titles, in the same year—something very few builders have done. As an older small man in a time of enormous young ones, he wanted badly to do it; though nobody gave him much of a chance against Mike Katz, who is one of the biggest of the young ones. Ed was giving away over half a foot in height, seventy pounds, and ten inches in the chest. Also, Mike was coming in very cut up, in his best shape ever, and wanting the contest with a fury. He had placed an embarrassing third the year before in Paris when it was supposed to be his year. Now this was supposed to be his year.

Baghdad, Iraq

"You want a drink first?" Mike asked, finally coming to life.

"Sure," said Corney. He got up and wrapped a shabby hotel towel around his middle and went over to the basin that was in the room and washed his face, splashing water over his penny-colored chest and shoulders. "We've just got two hours. Weider says to be at the Cinema right at four. What's the story on using oil?"

"Can't use it," I told Ed. "The judges have declared it illegal."

Corney shrugged. His skin is naturally dark, with good bright tone. He would not miss using the baby oil in the contest as much as some. Like Katz, for instance, whose chalky skin needs the oil to bring out definition under the posing spot.

Mike grunted. He was set to anticipate that kind of news over here, a half-Jew in a crazy little Arab country where all his friends and his wife had told him he was nuts to come; he had been set ever since he got here for anything from having the oil banned on him to being sniped at from a roof, but so far the Iraqis had treated him with pure and simple idolatry, leaving him very little to grunt that way about. He got up to make one of the viscous protein drinks that he and Ed drank three times a day to ease their worries about the food.

Two and a half hours ago for lunch they had eaten a bowl of thin, unidentifiable soup, four well-done kebab patties made of ground meat and grain, and four eggs apiece. It *looked* safe, sure, and it tasted OK. But in bodybuilding, intake—the transference of liquids and solids to amino acids to proteins to muscle tissue—is half the ball game, and you don't take all that weird Arabic bread and dirty-looking fruit lightly. For lunch at home Mike would have had a pound and a half of lean ground round, cottage cheese, an apple or orange juice and a protein drink with eight ounces of milk, four eggs and six tablespoons of protein blended into it. That would make up about a third of the three to four hundred grams of protein he consumes every day, and make it up safely. But the only part of all that stuff you could bring with you to Baghdad was the protein powder.

He did have that. He opened his closet and looked at it, a huge can of Blair "Rheo-H" Protein Supplement, sitting on a shelf at the center of the other cans and bottles he and Corney had brought over with them. In addition to the protein, there were Weider Bone-Plus Vitamin D, Weider Super-B Concentrate, Weider 300-Milligram Vitamin C, Weider Brewer's Yeast and Iron, Weider Multi-Vitamin Mineral 100, Weider Supreme E Formula R3, and a can of Blair "Rheo-H" Choline Plus, for the proper digestion of fat.

Mike took down the can of protein and carried it over to the basin. He pried off the top and took down the big blender cup they used for mixing.

They did have the powder, all right. But there was a story

Mike Katz
2972-72 IFBB Mr. America, 1912-
1B IFBB Mr. World
29 years old
6'1" tall
240 lbs.
58" chest
21" arms
31" waist
29" thighs
18" calves

"You know my whole life seems —and I'm not feeling sorry for myself, but Nancy knows, she's been with me all my life—it always seems, I don't know whether it's because I've got a Jewish name or what it is, but it always seems like people have picked on me. You know—always trying to find fault with me. Constantly not giving me credit. Right from when I started playing peewee baseball, you know. I could throw a ball faster, I could run faster, I could do different things better, but I'd never start off—you know, play the whole game. And I always had that damn feeling as a youngster. You know I think sometimes that maybe why I'm doing what I'm doing is to get back at some . . . I don't know whether it's unconscious, but just to show the world, those people that made fun of me . . . and I was bullied quite a bit when I was a kid too, you know. It's a funny thing but I can re-member and it sounds really weird: I had this bike. It was a real nice bike, you know. Kids are impressed with bikes when they're young—that's the big thing. And I can remember the fenders of the bike getting rusty. I never told anybody this. And I can remember the kids bothering me. Oh, man. Just bothering me about it. And another thing. I couldn't read that well, you know, and I had eye problems. And you know how kids can be really mean. My eyes sometimes crossed. I had two operations and the kids used to make fun of my eyes. And they used to make fun of the bumpers on my bicycle. Little

Baghdad airport

around that the water they had to mix it with might have, *could* have, in it these tiny little invisible snaillike things that could get into your bloodstream and. . . .

Things untellably strange and a certain amount of free-floating anxiety about them had been a part of this trip from the beginning. Bodybuilding contests themselves are exotic; but when you talk about pulling one together with contestants, delegates and press from thirty-two countries, and holding it in the city of Sheherazade, as the central event of five national days of banquets and bodybuilding-executive meetings and excursions to Babylon and down the Tigris River, and about preceding the whole deal with a thing called a Mr. Universe-in-Transit Ball in Geneva, Switzerland—you are talking then about something happening out on the farthest fringe of possibility.

Mike Katz is no dummy. He knows before most people do when things feel weird. He pointed to something printed in Arabic letters over the escape door in the big green-and-white Iraqi National Airlines chartered jet warming up to take us from Geneva to Baghdad by way of Athens—at least two of which places he had never either expected or wanted particularly to see.

"Do you guys know what that says?" he boomed to the plane load of French, Argentines, Belgians, Dutch, Welsh, Brazilians, Spanish, Finns, Canadians, Swedes, Americans, Swiss, and an eccentric Hawaiian named Dr. You who kept claiming loudly that he could create a world champion at anything within a week and that he had turned down five million dollars for the secret

Hotel Baghdad

of how to send a woman into space.

"What that says," Mike told them, only half joking, "is 'sucker' in Arabic."

The plane began to taxi. The pilot announced in English where we hoped to go and how long it would take, his voice vibrating like a sitar string in the high-pitched Middle Eastern accent that the whole world has come to associate with various kinds of airplane disasters. And all those huge men went quiet. They stopped talking the six or seven languages they had been talking and went suddenly big-eyed and pacific as children—over the Alps to Baghdad? in a green-and-white Iraqi plane with Arabic writing all over it, with a dude that sounds like that—more conscious than most, because of their size and strength, of gravity; and probably wanting more than most to arrive wherever the hell it was they were going, even if it was Oz, all of a piece, the parts still relating with some art to the whole.

And there was nothing about the way we were met at 2 a.m. at the airport in Baghdad to make Mike or anybody else feel any more at ease with things—greeted as we were by a cadre of small, swart, officious men in military uniforms and clipped mustaches, a few even with swagger sticks, who plied everyone with coffee, hurried their bags through customs, and created deferential little ceremonies for them all through the airport as though they were greeting a group of Russian economists instead of a planeful of bodybuilders.

That was the main thing out of joint, then and for the next four days. For Mike Katz and Ed Corney, and many of the other

things. And like there was a lady in school, she was a guidance teacher whose name was Mrs. Bassett. Nancy remembers. And she told me that I would never be able to become a college graduate, that it was impossible, that I just didn't have the intelligence and I should take up Industrial Arts. And man, you know from that peewee coach in baseball knocking me to the people in school. . . . I used to cry. In seventh grade I can remember the math teacher used to make fun of me and be sarcastic, and the reading teacher used to put me in the rottenest reading group. Man! You know those things I can remember as a kid did a helluva lot to make me push and show everybody what I could do. I think that's probably one of the, you know, had a lot to do with me wanting to achieve the greatness I want to achieve, just to say, 'Hey, look at me now,' you know. 'You made fun of me then, but look what I turned into...' They used to call me Porky too. That was another thing they used to make fun of."
—Mike Katz

"Well, most people think that bodybuilders are strictly after their body in appearance only. I find that that isn't true. That's only half of it. The other half is it comes on rather strong in developing yourself mentally as well. A broad outlook on life— the trials and tribulations, ups and downs, you know. You're able to take things as they come and go."
—Ed Corney

builders, it was as if they had suddenly passed through a time warp—out of a place where they were unknown and snickered at, where their highest accomplishments were assumed to be deviant and freakish and where they had learned to live with all that, and into one where bodybuilding was the second most popular sport and where they were instantly recognizable heroes. Like Muhammad Ali or Hank Aaron. Even like Joe Namath.

"Meek Kitz?" said one little military man in an awed voice. He was beaming up at Mike, his wild Arab eyes spinning. "Ahhhhhg . . . Meek Kitz. Welcome, Meek Kitz, to you *and to all champions*."

Katz stared hard at the man. Nothing in the other place had prepared him for this moment. But he had played on the same football team with Namath. And he did know to grab it while it was there. He could wonder about what it all meant later; worry then about whether or not there was anything sinister going on. So he smiled, with truly graceful largesse, and said,
"Thank you. It's a pleasure to be here."

For the next two days he and Ed Corney went right on smiling like that through one indecipherable but pleasant situation after another: on the dusty streets where they were followed and beleaguered by hordes of men and children shoving papers at them to sign, the retinue growing as they walked, so that after four or five blocks there might be thirty people winding behind them through the strange streets that swarmed with robed men and veiled women, with bicycles, pushcarts and 1953 Chevrolets; or down the stone alleyways of the medieval *suks*, the ancient

The Mayor of Baghdad's tent

copper, silver and gold bazaars in Old Baghdad whose stunning Elizabethan raunchiness of crowded smells and noises, of texture laid on texture, of cramped, shrill ripeness bounded by treacherous shadows and decay, lay over and smeared all their perceptions like Vaseline on a camera lens.

And at lunch on Sunday, the day after we arrived, at the Al-Mansoon Racing Club with chief delegates from various national bodybuilding federations—strange-looking, bulky men in tight suits from places like Pakistan and Kuwait, Thailand and Turkey, many of them fingering worry beads. The club was an airy second-story room bordered by a terrace that overlooked an enormous beturbanned crowd, and beyond it to an emerald-green mile-and-a-half track where there were races going on. Vendors down below in the crowd sold slices of melon and cups of thick, bitter coffee. The jockeys rode magnificent Arabian horses and wore long bright silk plumes on their helmets that streaked behind them in races against the hot blue sky. Lunch was a mammoth buffet of whole twenty-pound fish, a side of lamb on a bed of yellow rice, chickens, the wheat circles full of meat called kibbie, sausages, beans with lamb, fruit cakes and custards. The Eastern delegates were the first at it, using their hands to tear off meat and serve their plates; and when everyone else was through, the servers and army drivers formed a line on either side of the table and savaged what was left, shoveling it into their mouths with both hands. Mike and Ed and the few other bodybuilders there ate as though they were picking lint off a lapel. They stood with their backs to walls, smiled steadily, and gazed out over the heads of the delegates at the bright races on the track.

Or at the prejudging for the short class which was held the next day on a lovely, cool, darkening late afternoon at El-Shaab Hall. After the posing, when everyone had looked over the small but very chiseled and worked Belgian, the big smooth South American with the heavy waist, and the nearly perfect Japanese and Egyptian who would take one and three in the class, they retired to an oval trellised garden outside the hall, bodybuilders and managers in sweat suits mingling and chatting quietly with the delegates and officials as if at tea on a Kensington lawn. At the center of the garden was a stone terrace. At the center of the terrace was a red inclined bench and three silver barbells; and somehow they looked perfectly natural out there, correct and dignified as a ship in a bottle at a yachting party. Ed Corney stood for a while at the edge of the terrace looking at the bench and the weights, dealing with them through the easy air as symbols, objects of respect—wagging his head and smiling.

And maybe especially at the dinner later that night given by the mayor of Baghdad for over three hundred people at Al-Zawrah Park. Held outside, under canopies and the stars, with illuminated pools between the buffet tables and fountains

"I want to be bigger than everybody else, but I wouldn't want to be so big that people can't accept it. For instance, if you come in with 30-inch arms, even your own peers aren't going to accept that. I wouldn't want to be that way. I wouldn't want to infinitely become unreal."
—Mike Katz

splashing and colored lights strung between poles—it was as festive and cordial as a Charleston debutante party. And Ed and Mike were there at the center of things, receiving compliments and eating carefully, shaking hands with endless foreign well-wishers, wondering at it all, and grinning their heads off.

Mike Katz stirred six tablespoons of protein powder into a full blender cup of the suspect water. He took some vitamin pills, chased them with half the mixture and gave the other half to Ed Corney. Then he took from a drawer *Le Maillot Culturiste* posing trunks he uses for contests, wrapped them carefully in a towel and stuck them in his gym bag for later.

"Let's get some sun," he said. "How much time we got?"

"Hour and a half until we have to be there. We can lie up there for an hour anyway," said Ed. "You guys coming up?" he asked me and George.

"How do you feel?" Mike asked him.

"Great. A little edgy. How about you?"

"Good," said Mike. "I feel good. But I wish it was over and we were back in the States. God, would I garbage up. What are you going to do over here? You gonna garbage up on those sheep's heads we saw boiling out in the street?"

Corney combed his black hair in the mirror and chuckled. They each had on workout trunks and sandals, and each of them had two towels to lie on up on the hot tile roof.

"You know they're televising this thing?" said Ed, putting down the comb. "It's going to be carried all over Iraq."

Mike Katz held the door open for him, smiling again, wide awake now, ready for anything. "Not just Iraq," he said. "They're showing it all over the Middle East."

Four

Serious training to a competitive bodybuilder means four things — exercising, eating, sleeping and tanning; and for as long as six months before a contest these four things are practically all he does. The last is separate from the others and important only to white builders; but as a way of giving the skin color and uniform finish under the lights, it is very important to them.

The other three are connected inside the body in a lovely mysterious machinery known as anabolism—the process by which simple substances are synthesized into the complex materials of living tissue. Anabolism is constructive metabolism, and "Metabolism" comes from the Greek word for change. Constructive change is what bodybuilding is all about. Simply put (because there is no better way to put it; like every process and fact of the human body it is beautiful and moving beyond language and can only be oversimplified as I am about to, or overcomplicated as physiologists do), it works like this: heavy, orchestrated exercise tears down the tissue of the muscles, and sleep and diet combine to replace and rebuild it, producing new and stronger flesh.

In any of the first-rate bodybuilders the three parts of this relationship are as finely adjusted, one to the others, as the main springs in a Piccard watch; and the result of that adjustment is a near-total control over the physical proportions—a protean capacity to manipulate weight and spaces by fractions of pounds or inches. That is a capacity unique in all the world to bodybuilders, as is the particular intimacy it gives them with their bodies.

Of the three, sleeping is the easiest to handle correctly. All you have to do is know exactly how much sleep is right for you

"Listen, I've been on countless TV shows, given countless lectures, and traveled all over the country for nothing, on behalf of youth groups and other organizations, just to try to change the image of what people thought a muscle man or bodybuilder was. But they all would say, 'Well, fine, great; there's ripples, there's lumps—that's, you know, what for?' A lot of people who have been honest with me have told me that there's an insecurity being around someone who's physically overpowering."
—Steve Michalik

Steve Michalik

and then manage to get it every day. I've known a few good builders who got by on four or five hours. Joe Disco sometimes went for weeks on that. Another one I know needs twelve. He swears that he can hear himself growing during the last three and that the sound is like Cornflakes being poured into a bowl. The exercising part is trickier. It takes a builder a long time to learn which ones are best for him, how best to mix and split them, when to increase or decrease weight and reps, and all the other thousand things he has to know to get the most from his workouts. But the hardest of the three to control with accuracy is eating. It is hardest because it allows the most room for mistakes and because of the truly bewildering variety of growth-producing foods, pills, powders, liquids and drugs that can be ingested.

The basics are simple enough: even a beginning bodybuilder knows to eat numerous small meals during a day instead of one or two big ones in order to avoid systemic and digestive overload —meals that are long on necessary vitamins, and protein foods like meat, cheese and eggs, and short on starches, fats and sugars. So he does that, and maybe takes a few supplemental vitamins, and drinks a protein drink at night made, maybe, out of Tiger's Milk, protein powder, peanut butter, two raw eggs and soybean oil, and he thinks he is doing everything right. But then some guy in the gym mentions that his tendons would be stronger if he ate a little kelp or dulse for the chlorine in it; or suggests he stop eating all that chard because too much sodium is building up his water table. Or he read that Franco Columbu takes vitamin E with vitamin A *before* meals, and B-complex with hydrochloric acid during them; or that Steve Michalik used to take two hundred desiccated liver tablets a day.

He hears about something called panothenic acid that he can find in crude molasses; and biotin, a dynamite vitamin in yeast. He learns about cold-pressed wheat germ oil for increasing stamina and reducing stretch marks; lecithin, for thinning cholesterol; predigested liquid proteins; shark liver oil; choline and inositol for getting rid of subcutaneous fat and bringing out cuts; nicotinic acid, for metabolizing the sugars he is not supposed to eat and preventing pellagra; and cobalamin, or vitamin B-I2, which will help increase his appetite for all this stuff. By now he is long out of basics. Nothing is simple anymore.

He finds out quickly that it is not only confusing but expensive to eat the way he is supposed to, that he will have to spend enough on food—just plain *food*, let alone all the pills and powders and things—to support two or three ordinary people.

Take Steve Michalik, for instance. Michalik is a chatty, sensitive, self-conscious man with a quick mind, a feel for publicizing himself, and a kinky love-hate relationship with body building. He is coming back to competition now after a two-year retirement, but he despises the demands it makes on him and his wife—not least the fact that for a year before he won the 1972 AAU Mr. America title she had to eat every meal with her mother because Michalik's food alone was running them seventy dollars a week. To gas up his anabolism every morning he would eat for breakfast two cube steaks, a sixteen-ounce can of tuna fish, cottage cheese, three or four hard-boiled eggs and a quarter pound of yellow cheese, and follow all that with a protein drink. Then two hours later he would eat again: a whole chicken, water-soluble vegetables, four hard-boiled eggs, more cottage cheese. Another drink. Pills. He forced himself through six of these meals a day.

He was working then as a commercial artist in Manhattan and he was lucky enough to have a boss who was fascinated with the great sea changes going on in Michalik. The boss bought him a grill, a hotplate, a blender and a refrigerator to facilitate his eating at the office. He bought him a lounge chair to sleep in for two hours each day, and he did not mind the hours of work Steve missed because he was training. This made things easier, but no less expensive. Nobody knows better than Michalik the various costs and difficulties of becoming a Mr. America. He nearly went broke and almost lost his marriage while doing it. And nobody knows better than he how little that title is worth on the open market. But if you ask him about it today, now that he blames bodybuilding for ruining his life, he'll tell you he would have eaten grease out of a crankcase at a dollar an ounce to have won it.

There is a part of this intake aspect of bodybuilding training that is not only complex and expensive but controversial, murky, widely lied about, and used by a lot of people to criticize the sport. It is the use of various drugs, mostly synthetic hormones, and it is much more talked about than it is understood. There are stories around about builders snorting coke and dropping reds and Dexedrine for energy. Maybe some do; I've never seen it or heard about it from anyone who knew what he was talking about, and the same is true with the stories you hear about guys getting their calves or arms shot up with silicone in Mexico. If these things happen, they happen with a very small percentage of builders and with virtually none of the best ones. Some body builders do try thyroid and pituitary shots for a while to step up their metabolisms, but most of them find that the shots don't really do that much and stop. But the drugs that draw the most attention and the most flak are the anabolic steroids, and there is no question that practically all first-class competitive body builders do use or have used them.

Steroids are synthetic testosterone, a principal male hormone produced in the testes that affects secondary sex characteristics. They are used medically to treat protein depletions, arthritis, geriatric problems and anemia, and to

"Then there's the off days. You're stuck with this off day, right? Well what are you going to do with the off day? Well I might as well do my calves. And I might as well do my waistline. I might as well do my forearms. I might as well do incidentals. I might as well work on definition. I might as well work on posing. You know, I might as well run to the library and learn more about what I should be eating at this particular time. Learn about metabolism, you know. And meanwhile while I'm doing this, there's my wife sitting home going bananas. And my mother, the clergy at the church and everyone saying, you know: 'What are you doing.? Take a day off.' I say, okay, fine. Sundays I'm going to rest. Sundays I find myself doing one-legged calf-raises on a street corner somewhere. Because when I'm up on that stage, I'm there by myself. Me alone. I'm not up there with a baseball bat. I'm not up there with a football. I'm there with just me. My body."
—Steve Michalik

help people recover from long sicknesses. They are also used to beef up cattle, and are known bleakly to give acne to women. The bodybuilders, weight lifters, wrestlers, football players, track men in the weight events, and other athletes who use them, do so because they believe they make them heavier and stronger. Whether or not they actually do is still in court. Of eleven recent controlled studies, six found that weight and strength are increased by the drugs, five found that they are not. The researcher in charge of the most recent of these studies is Dr. Larry Golding of Kent State University. Golding probably knows as much about the relation of steroids to sport as any man in the country, and it is his belief and the finding of his study that steroids cannot make anyone bigger or stronger except by a touching psychological mechanism known as the placebo effect—believing in the drug so strongly that belief produces the results that the drug is supposed to produce.

Regardless of what Dr. Golding and other scientists find in laboratories, most bodybuilders believe that they cannot build themselves beyond a certain point without steroids, and that to stay competitive they have to use them. But they don't like doing it (they usually deny that they do until you get to know them well, and are quick to point out that if steroids were all it took, any Jack on the street could make himself a Mr. Olympia with just a prescription), and they will stop on a dime or cut down, as Arnold Schwarzenegger did over a year ago, when they are convinced they can get along without them.

They don't like using them partly because it lays them and the sport open to the use-one-use-them-all criticism often insinuated by people who don't know any better, that bodybuilding is rife with junkies. And because of the unsubstantiated but ubiquitous rumors about how the drugs can ruin your liver or make you go bald, or even wither up your balls. But mostly they don't like using them because they sense that in an oblique way doing so gives some weight to one of the most abhorred of all the many public discomforts about them: that all those muscles somehow come out of a bottle; that there is something as synthetic, unhealthy, useless and faintly sinful as plastic flowers about what they do and the way they look—as though all the discipline, sacrifice and work of their training, and the organic balance of exercise, fueling and rest that has to be found and struck exactly right inside the body before the outside becomes a proper medium, and the sane, satisfying connection between the body's health and its beauty, and how good they feel all the time, how good the lungs feel, and the skin, and how they can almost hear the blood circulate, and how easily they can move themselves and other things —as though all those things counted for nothing, could be reduced to something the size of a pill.

Dr. Golding himself wondered. He had run physiological tests on other athletes, regular athletes, at his applied-physiology research center in Kent, but never on one of these blown-up fellows. Did their training, he wondered, put them "in shape," or was all that muscle the result of some dark pill alchemy and as useless as so much cotton batting under the skin? So through Ben Weider, president of the International Federation of Bodybuilders, he got himself an invitation to Baghdad, where he met Mike Katz, and a month or two after the contest he had Katz come out to Kent State to undergo a battery of tests. He dunked Mike in tubs of water, took skin-fold and body measurements, had him ride a stationary bicycle, and counted his pulse over and over. What he found was that Katz was phenomenally fit; every one of his scores was in the superior rating except for his sitting heart rate, which was a high good; he was only eleven percent fat, five percent below normal, his subcutaneous fat was practically nonexistent, and his cardiovascular system and aerobic capacity were spectacular.

But the most telling fact was the result of the bicycle-ride test that measured Mike's physical-work capacity (PWC). What it told is all anybody needs to know about a world-class bodybuilder's training. The test determined that Mike's maximum work load was 2,400 KPM. That meant that his PWC was completely off the scale they used to measure it.

"I was interested in the beauty of the male physique, and showing the beauty of the male physique to whoever had paid to come to see it. So I would move to music, and pose, and do sort of ballet, and go down and twist and forward, just so it looked . . . it would look almost like if you looked at a lion running through the jungle. Sometimes if you can catch a lion, or a horse or a doe—they're so beautiful just the way they move. And I would try to incorporate this in my posing. Definitely not putting any real muscley, veiny type poses in there, because I didn't want to turn anyone off. I just wanted to bring the beauty of the male physique across. Because I really feel that the male physique is just as beautiful if not more beautiful than the female's. Now horses, the male is prettier. Male lion. The peacock. I love women and everything. But, well, look at me. I just feel that a man has as much to offer as a woman."

—Steve Michalik

Five
Mr. Universe No. 2

It was hot on the roof. The sky was the same parched blue it was every day from dawn to sunset—a dusty, deserty blue—and the sun lay across the width of it like varnish on a windowpane. Few of the noises drifting up from below sounded real. And whenever Mike Katz or Ed Corney stood up, wandered to the edge of the roof and looked out into the teeming streets, or over the random sprawl of blocky sand-colored buildings to minarets and palm trees on an aquamarine horizon, not much looked real either. It all seemed like—ahh, well, like a movie. Particularly since the whole city was so tuned in to them. It was almost as if all the noise and movement down there on the streets was for them in a funny way—as if they were the central characters in a fantasy, like kings of Mardi Gras.

Right at that moment, for instance, wasn't Hussarian, their assigned chauffeur, a shy, unctuous student of English from the University of Baghdad whose eyes could not have been directed by John Huston to spin with more awe whenever he looked at them—wasn't good old Hussarian just inside the roof door over there keeping back a ragged horde who would cheerfully have stood swaddled in bearskins on the steaming roof just to watch Meek Kitz and Et Carney catch a few rays? Who knew? It could have been thousands, half of Baghdad, that Hussarian was holding off—clutching a scimitar or something, his soft eyes gone hard with purpose.

As the afternoon wore on toward four, Ed Corney and Mike Katz flipped themselves over occasionally, sweated freely in private stews of images and nerves, and tried not to think about the contest. They had each dreamed the night before that the other

"Why does this particular thing turn people off? I believe that people should be built the way I'm built. I don't think people should walk around looking like a piece of junk. I've got normal clothes on—if they fit tight maybe it's because I can't afford clothes that don't fit tight. I don't have anything showing that shouldn't be showing. Some guys walk around really freaky, but that turns me off too. When I go to the beach I have these little areas where nobody goes but seagulls. Nobody bothers me. I want to compete—I want to be the greatest in the world. If that's wrong, it's wrong."
—Mike Katz

Mike Katz, hulking the lineup

"Sometimes when you're working out in the gym and you're so much more developed and, you know, unbelievable in comparison to anybody working out around you, you say to yourself, 'Man, am I real? Is it possible that I really am this big?' And sometimes, you know, I'll gander at the mirror when I'll see some little guy who's working pretty hard go by and I'll say, 'That's ridiculous; how can this be possible?' Then I start, sometimes I find myself looking for defects in the mirror, you know, to see if I'm really that big or if there may be a mistake—you know, a wave in the mirror that makes you look bigger. I don't get hung up thinking about it, but sometimes I do. You know you're not normal, because normal is 6 feet tall, 150 or 160 pounds, you know, fairly skinny; or a big fat person. So that you know that because you're superiorly built, and you've trained and developed that way, that you do look odd. I mean, you do look unreal."
—Mike Katz

Prejudging

one would win the Mr. Universe title. If there was ever a place that seemed right for taking omens seriously, this place had to be it, and neither one of them liked his dream very much. Also, they had seen each other pose that morning at the prejudging for their height classes and determined privately, as everybody else had, that the overall title had to go to one of them; but also that it could go to either one.

Mike had had no serious competition in the tall class. He looked very confident in the lineup, vastly bigger than anyone else and even more cut up than he had been in New York a couple of months before when he beat Ken Waller for the Mr. World. There was a heavily muscled Iraqi with less calf even than Mike in the line, and a smooth symmetrical Spaniard named Baldo Lois; but the rest of the class was like the two doe-eyed Palestinians who looked like brothers and went everywhere together holding hands—serious but hopeless, five or six light-years away from Mike Katz. Mike had hulked them bad in the lineup—wearing himself like armor, waiting until they were already into their poses before he hit his, and making sure all of them saw that if he decided to spread his lats, he could hide any two of them. Corney's class, the mediums, had been better. A Swede, a Frenchman, a Belgian and the Iraqi had all looked good, and any one of them could have won the class if he had not had the bad luck of having Ed Corney in it with him. Relaxed, inside himself, staring as he always does at a point on the back wall of the gallery, he had a tight density of presence in the line that made him seem the only one in it. And he posed flawlessly, flowing purely as water from shot to shot in that quietly dramatic way of his that emphasizes the perfect balance and clarity of his muscles—not knocking people over with his size the way Katz does, not even flexing, really, so much as arranging the muscle groups in smooth serpentine shifts that surprise and gratify as you watch. It is a balletic kind of posing that no one does as well as he. Frank Zane, another major bodybuilder with a similar style, makes it look too soft and choreographed; with Corney every movement is virile, spontaneous and pure. By the end of the morning both of them knew that they would win their classes, all right; and that they had only each other to worry about for the title. But after watching each other pose, that had seemed like more than enough.

Around three-thirty they left the heat and images on the roof and went back to their room to get ready. Hussarian came along.

"Iss time to go," he suggested as soon as Ed had shut the door.

"Relax," Mike told him. Which was exactly what he and Ed then proceeded to do. Back in the room with familiar rituals to perform, nothing weird to look at or hear, and with the contest too close to think about, both of them nerved out, went calm, and began enjoying themselves.

Talking and clowning, Mike stood in front of a mirror and gave his arms, legs and chest a quick final shave with an injector razor. Then he covered them with a light coat of Tan-in-a-Minute, feathering the stuff out with his palms so it would leave no lines, and got Ed to rub some of it into his back. After the lotion had dried he rubbed a thin, expert film of baby oil over it, and then checked himself over in the mirror, looking very carefully at his red-bronze, glinting surface.

Hussarian had watched all this with a vague, stoned expression on his face like a baby watching fire, and it wasn't until Mike was completely finished with himself and dressing that he returned enough to notice that the contest was due to start in five minutes. "*Sheeeeet*," he said simply.

"Whassat, Hussarian, old buddy?" asked Ed, who had dressed quickly in jeans and a wild blue-and-white Hawaiian shirt and had been ready for minutes. He knew we were all going to be late but hadn't mentioned it because the last twenty minutes had been fun, and most of all loose, and there wasn't a lot of that around this place. "What's eating you?"

"We go now," said Hussarian, scuttling over to Katz. "Eeeeeeii . . . *we go now quickly, Meek Kitz*," he pleaded.

Katz looked at him, then at Corney, then at me, his lean face serious and quizzical. He had just been combing his hair, for God's sake. Now what was this little-mother act?

"We're running a little short on time," Ed told him. "Hussarian's worried about it. Why don't you ask him can he whip out a flying carpet?"

The suggestion didn't even sound facetious. I mean for kings of Mardi Gras? Why the hell not?

Ben Weider was more than just mad; he was pale around the lips and quivering when the American team arrived at the Al-Nasr Cinema twenty minutes late.

"You have *missed*," he told them, "the international march. There was no one to carry in the American flag."

We had come in through the backstage door of the Cinema, which houses the largest auditorium in the Middle East, and the corridors were a bedlam of rocketing Arabs, photographers, half-dressed contestants, and people with IFBB badges trying to tell everyone else what to do. Beyond the stage over two thousand people were packed into the seats and standing spaces of the auditorium, and there were at least another thousand outside milling, making mad rushes at the door, and reaching plaintively through the bars on the building's windows, only to have their arms rapped methodically by the billies of officials standing inside. With all the noise and confusion, and with at least a half-dozen pairs of small dark hands clutching at each of them, it was very difficult for Ed and Mike to pay attention, even to the enraged president of the International Federation of Bodybuilders.

Mr. Sweden, Mr. France, Mr. America

"He [Ed Corney] has a slightly
more finished physique than I
do. He's a little rounder. You
know, he's got no weak points
and my arms could be slightly
bigger. My calves could be bigger.
And his physique—he's not over-
whelming; he's not huge or dynamic as far as his physique
goes. But he's just very symmetrical. You look to try to find flaws
in him and there's just very, very
little you can find."
—Mike Katz

Oiling up

"What?" one of them asked him.

"You are late, you are very, very horribly *late*. The international march is over and the short class is already on stage. *Where have you been?*"

"We were dressing," Ed told him. "Where do we change?"

Just then a frantic-looking Iraqi official came tearing around a corner wringing his hands and crying hysterically at the backs of two South American builders, "*Noaisllle, noaisllle, noaisllle...*"

It was a horrible, keening statement that might have been announcing rape, fire—any one of a dozen disasters. And like the dreams, and the being late, it was mighty like an omen. Whatever it was, it stunned the backstage into near silence.

"What's he saying?" asked Mike Katz. "This place has gone crazy."

As Ben Weider began to hustle him and Ed through the crowd to the dressing room, both hands full of their triceps, Hussarian sidled up to Mike.

"He say no *aisle*." Hussarian rubbed his chest. "It iss not allowed for champions to use aisle on the body." "Oh," said Mike.

"Oh, yeah." But he wasn't really listening anymore. He was finally getting ready to do what he came here to do, what he had waited and trained for a year to do. And he didn't care if everybody else in this fantasy went stark raving crazy.

Serge Nubret at the Lion of Babylon

Six
Mr. Olympia No. 2

Over in the sandy general-exercise area there are men and women climbing ropes and working out on balance beams and parallel bars. Pickup games of basketball, volleyball and soccer are going on, and from where the beach begins to the loud dirty Pacific fifty yards away, as far as you can see in either direction, is knee deep with people. Stationed along the bicycle path above the beach are delicate little concrete tables, and at one of them a Saturday luncheon party of winos dreams out over all of this, taking the sun.

Between the paddle-tennis courts and the basketball is the weight-lifting platform and beside it a bright green sward of grass with a lot of big men in small bathing suits lying around. This is bodybuilders' turf: their piece of Venice Beach, as separate from the rest of it as Gold's Gym is. It is around two o'clock on Monday, the outside, digestive part of the day between morning and afternoon workouts. There are a few middle-aged builders out, old-timers from the days of Muscle Beach, with their young wives and babies and small waists. A couple of girl friends. A doctor who specializes in nutrition. A powerlifter in a wheelchair with enormous arms and no legs. And a girl bodybuilder with a big dog named Oberline. The rest are guys from Gold's who are getting ready for New York and to whom this tanning is serious business, almost as important a part of their day as training or eating. All of them but one lie as stiff as corpses, moving only to turn.

The other one is Arnold Schwarzenegger. He sits at the center of things in a bright-orange brief, shades, and a borrowed wide-brim straw hat, a downtown hat—mimicking black jive talk

"There are some girls who are turned on by my body, and some others who are turned off. But for the majority I just use it as a conversation piece. Like someone walking a cheetah down 42nd Street would have a natural conversation piece. Then when they get to talking to me they see I am not mean but gentle to them and that's all they want to know."
—Arnold Schwarzenegger

Arnold and fans

Franco

"When a homosexual looks at
a bodybuilder, I don't have any
thing against that. I would probably stare the same way if Raquel
Welch or Brigitte Bardot walked
by. If I see a girl with big tits,
I'm going to stare and stare. And
I'm going to think in my mind
what I'm going to do with her if
I would have her. The same is
true with the homosexual—he's
looking at the bodybuilder and
picturing what he would do
with him. You have to face it
if you have a good body, and it
is somehow a compliment to a
bodybuilder. Sometimes girls are
attracted to your body; sometimes
homosexuals are attracted to your
body."
—Arnold Schwarzenegger

Arnold and Franco with George Butler
Photograph by Joe Welder

"I have a good sense of my body in a bathing suit around people who appreciate what I'm doing, like a contest. Then I'm proud. On television I am proud. But on a beach most people are not experts. The general public doesn't know how to look. How proud can you be when they don't even know what they're looking at?"
—Arnold Schwarzenegger

with his deep, Nazi voice.

"Goawnn, Arnold," says the owner of the hat, cracking up.

Spurred, Arnold begins a series of imitations, getting each exactly, and devastating the girl on Denny Gable's back. She sits astride Gable in a bikini, rubbing coconut oil into his shoulders, playing dust to Arnold's vacuum cleaner. Evidently she walked into this cold; she is not one of the groupies who hang around here—like the carnivorous-eyed males lolling nearby with cameras around their necks—just to get a glimpse of him. Nobody told her she was going to run into one of the most magnetic men in the Western world today, and she is fairly humming. But Arnold is used to that. There's nothing new there and it doesn't affect his performance. Midway into it he decides he needs oil himself and he asks Kent Kuehn for some. Kuehn, prone on his stomach, mutters into the grass that he doesn't have any.

Arnold shakes his head solemnly. "They all haff it in the back of their minds, these guys, to knock off the King," he says.

Just then, into the thick of this, from somewhere out of the California afternoon wanders an alligator wrestler from Florida with a knife at his hip, looking, perhaps, like a real assassin. He seats himself carefully on the bodybuilders' grass, crosses his legs, and only then looks around—plaintively at first like a hit dog, his eyes whirling with dope; but then as he begins to focus on these people around him, and particularly on the unreal one with the hat, this alligator wrestler, this typical segment of the outside world, commences hysterically and uncompromisingly to *stare*.

A few years ago some inventive psychology course somewhere ran an experiment in alienation in which a student was made to wear a paper bag over his head to class every day for a semester. At first the other students were amused by the bagged one, but after a few weeks he began to get mysteriously on their nerves, and by the end of the semester most of them confessed to feeling all-out hatred or terror for the sonofabitch in the sack.

There are as few men built even remotely like Arnold as there are, say, Przhevalski horses or Texas blind salamanders. And nothing in modern American life had prepared that gentle man from Florida for what he was confronted with. He found himself, suddenly and hideously, in the middle of a lawn full of people with bags over their heads, and all he knew to do was stare. He is not alone. Outside of the Gold's Gyms and Venice Beaches, almost the entire civilized world stares at bodybuilders, with disgust, with fright, with awe. And a few—like the girl who ran into Arnold in a bar the night before—with pure-D ecstasy. She was backing out of the place banging a tambourine, in the company of four or five other stagettes out for a night on the town, when she ran smack into the entering Arnold. He caught her. She turned to him, her head just above the level of his

waist, and began to feel him experimentally, as though he were the back wall of a cave. She felt, paused, felt a little higher. "Jesus Christ," she shrieked at her friends. "Come *feel* this. Look at this goddam body!"

Arnold might have told her, Look, I am the supreme example of an art form for which there is hardly an audience in this country. Or: What you are now feeling is a body, yes ma'am, but it is also an athletic product like Catfish Hunter's slider or Ken Rosewall's backhand, the result of years of disciplined and specialized training, that you could not possibly appreciate fully until you have seen it on a stage, doing what it does in competition.

He could have said something like that, but instead he just grabbed back. She knew how to look, this girl. And a body builder's whole world breaks cleanly as a saltine into those who know how to look and those who don't.

Opposite Page:
Top: Ben Welder with Oscar State
Bottom: Arnold and Joe Welder

Part Two
The Competition

Art completes what nature cannot bring to a finish.
The artist gives us a knowledge of nature's
unrealized ends.

—Aristotle

Bodybuilding as such is not really a sport at all.
It's a very serious performance of art, I believe.

—Sigmund Klein

Seven

If a sport is a physical activity that human beings train for in order to compete at, then bodybuilding is certainly a sport. And yet Sig Klein is right: more importantly and interestingly, it is also an art form; and one of the things that bother the millions who don't know how to look is a confusion over how and where these two meet. Since very few of those people have ever been to a body contest, they have no way to understand how having muscles can be a competitive thing; and since they live in a time when the male body is generally not regarded very highly, and practically never in aesthetic terms, it is just as difficult to imagine how it can be an artistic thing. They are used to sports where the body is a means, not an end in itself, and it seems effete to a lot of them for a sport to require nothing more of the body than just to be presented for viewing. "What are all those muscles good for? I mean what can those guys *do* with them?" are the sort of practical questions you hear.

The fact is they can usually do a lot of things with them; that is a fact but not the point. The point is that the nature of bodybuilding competition is aesthetic rather than athletic. There are other sports where artistic judgments determine the competition—like diving, and show riding, and figure skating, and free-style skiing. And there are still others, like tournament fly casting or skeet shooting, where the skills being tested are as divorced from their practical applications as a bodybuilder's muscles are from the work they can do. Bodybuilding is a little like those sports. In its stylization of movement and concern with ritual it is also a little like bullfighting. But largely it is unlike anything else, and to be really able to enjoy it, to learn

Charles Atlas posing for statue
(From the collection of Charles Roman)

103

"I'd wear a half leotard—sometimes I'd have a red one, I had different colors—and Roman sandals. And I did, first I'd do the muscle posing, classical posing; muscle control, uh, hand balanceing and then juggling of weights —kettle weights, dumbbells and barbells. First you take 'em and spin 'em—from left to right. Then you reverse 'em. Then a double spin. Then you throw it over your shoulder and catch it in front of you. . . . They'd weigh sometimes from 25 to 35 pounds, more heavier if you do 'em right. Then you take the kettle bell, throw it behind you and catch it over there. You go between your legs and spin and catch it here. And then you learn other little tricks with it. I'd often wind up by hanging it on my little finger and I'd have a kid hold a cardboard and I'd write my name, Klein, in black letters.

"All right. That was the kettle bell. Then with the dumbbell, you'd do other things. I'd swing it up, right? And I'd let it spin and catch it on the sphere. Now there'd be one sphere there on my hand, right; the other one's way up on top. From there I'd spin it and catch it on the handle, and then I'd throw it into this hand, then into that hand. Then I'd lei it drop into the crook of the arm. I'd spin it around, catch it here, and do that several times. Then I'd spin it in front of me this way. Then I'd lift it up and put it behind my head on the shoulders . . . and then tilt it off and spin it around real fast. And with a barbell . .. I'd often take the whole barbell and rest the sphere on the palm of the hand and then

how to look (if you don't just naturally know how like the stagette in the bar), it is helpful to begin with a couple of basic suppositions.

First, for anyone who would like one, here is a definition: contest bodybuilding is athletic training of the body for artistic competition. To enjoy or understand it you need to suppose, first, that the male body is a potentially beautiful thing, capable of being worked and perfected like a piece of sculpture, and, second, that the product of that work can be a serious subject for contemplation and visual enjoyment.

These may be unfashionable things to suppose, but they are not at all new. At certain periods of Western history they were taken for granted, and the two major peaks of our visual culture, the sculpture of fourth- and fifth-century-B.C. Greece, and the painting and sculpture of the Renaissance, were based on and inspired by a vision of the perfected male body as the single most articulate and satisfying form in nature. A similar vision, an imaged idea of the potential formal beauty of flesh, lies at the root of bodybuilding, both as sport and as art—from the time some skinny fourteen-year-old with Tareytons rolled into the sleeve of his T-shirt picks up his first barbell to make his arms a little bigger, until years of training later when, if he is very lucky and good and unsparing with himself, his body might come together in a certain pose and everyone watching will think he is seeing that particular configuration of the human form for the first time ever.

From the beginning a bodybuilder works with himself as a medium, in much the same way that Praxiteles or Phidias or Michelangelo worked with bronze and Carrara marble—formalizing and idealizing his material, dispensing with its imperfections and forcing an idea of it into design. In his work he is after the same basic qualities of balance and clarity that those artists were after, so it is not surprising that often the result of his work is strikingly like the sculpture and painting of classical and Renaissance artists.

The schematized architecture of abdominal, oblique, serratus and pectoral muscles developed by Polycleitus in the fifth century B.C. (which became so accepted a disposition of those muscles that it served as a model for the cuirasse, or torsopiece of armor) could have been lifted directly off Franco Columbu. In the Metropolitan Museum there is a Roman bronze of the Emperor Trebonianus Gallus whose rib cage and thighs look exactly like Mike Katz's, and a Hellenistic statue of the Drunken Herakles with a right leg like Ken Waller's. The Farnese Hercules statue in the National Museum in Naples, Michelangelo's figures of God and Adam on the ceiling of the Sistine Chapel, and his magnificent statue of Day on the tomb of Giuliano de' Medici, as well as any number of other works by

press it up slowly. And that was quite a balancing stunt—to hold that old barbell up there like that."
—Sig Klein

Sigmund Klein
73 years old
5'4 1/2" tall
148 lbs.

Siggy Klein, ca. 1925   Siggy Klein 1973

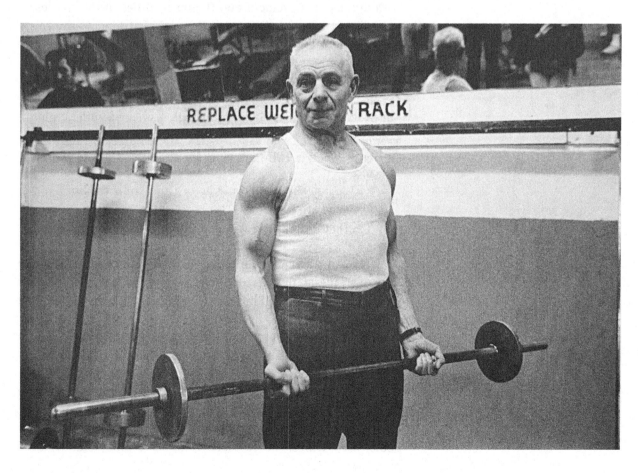

REPLACE WEIGHTS ON RACK

Hellenic, Hellenistic, Roman and Renaissance artists, look as though they might have been painted or sculpted using contemporary bodybuilders as models.

It is easy to make more out of these kinds of similarities than ought to be made. Franco Columbu has probably never heard of Polycleitus or a cuirasse, and I know for a fact that he doesn't think of himself as walking sculpture. The point is that, like the humanist artists of classical Greece and the Renaissance, he is involved in transforming the human anatomy into an instrument of expression; and that while his training is athletic (more gruelingly so than that for any other sport except maybe long-distance running), the product of it is not a speed or a skill but his own body, reorganized and rendered into something which has to be looked at and evaluated aesthetically to be appreciated, and which should be able to provide at least as much pleasure when studied that way as a piece of marble twenty-five centuries old that resembles it.

The problem for a lot of people in taking that pleasure, of course, has to do with the fact that Franco is made out of *flesh* —a stuff that pulls at our most intimate emotions and memories in a way marble can't. Those humanist artists, after all, weren't really sculpting or painting men, but Man, right? —at times in history when people believed in him—showing him muscular with dignity, achievement and the possibilities of the species. It was all sort of *symbolic*, and looking at that kind of thing is a damned sight different from looking at some raffish, beefed-up ex-bricklayer Sardinian.

"God, these guys are *gross*. I mean . . . *God*," she said.

She was a secretary at the William Morris Agency in New York City and she was looking through a stack of Butler's photographs which she had asked to see, turning them over one by one with a single two-inch fingernail as though they might be infected.

We had been this route before and knew the lines.

"Why are they gross?"

"Do they really look like this? I mean that's just . . . that's just . . ."

"How about sculpture? How about those Greek and Roman statues at the Metropolitan with all the muscles?" "That's different. That's aht." She finished the stack, sighed. "Aht isn't human."

Maybe not. But I can think of a number of times when it was very hard to tell the difference between them. Like one hot Sunday afternoon at the Mountain Park Amusement Center in Holyoke, Massachusetts. Outside the auditorium or pavilion as it is called, a roller coaster clattered up and down a wooden trestle. Children flew around on little whirly things that looked like boats with wings. There were clam bars, pizza stands, dart throws, cotton-candy booths and a Commando Machinegun stall. Inside, on the stage in front of twelve hundred people, Leon Brown, a black laundry worker from Staten Island, was posing for the 1972 Mr. East Coast title. He had come on stage in a high-chested glide, his mouth a little ajar, his eyes flat with concentration, and stared for a long moment into the rear of the huge auditorium as if somebody back there were trying to teach him canasta. Then he found whatever it was he was looking for and began a routine that was right on top of perfect. Somewhere toward the middle of it he slid into a back pose and jiggled it tense—trapezius, deltoid, infraspinatus, lats, all the workhorse muscles of the back, coming together suddenly like the click of a box and gleaming above his white posing trunks like oiled chocolate in perfect organized mounds. It was the kind of pose that a bodybuilder finds only once in a while—when everything is right and he reaches for it and hauls it down, and all the muscles fall into place like gears meshing. For the people in that audience it was like seeing Leon get hit by lightning.

Learning how to look at bodybuilding is probably no more than learning how to be objective and unembarrassed about the body, enough so that you could look at that back pose of Leon's without wondering about what makes him do it, or how it smells up there, or what his sex life is like—and just go along with the visual thrill of seeing something brilliant and uniquely expressive done with the human form.

As a preoccupation of men who have wanted to make themselves stronger, bodybuilding has been around since the Babylonians. But in its present sport-art, competitive form it is a relatively recent phenomenon that seems to have grown out of the nineteenth-century European strongman acts.

Nobody tells how that might have happened better than Sig Klein.

Sig Klein is seventy-three years old. He began bodybuilding in 1919, is still doing it, and is in better shape today than most men ever get into. When he retired from business two years ago to spend more time collecting beer mugs, he closed down one of the first, and oldest continually operating, bodybuilding gymnasiums in the country—a legendary place, on Seventh Avenue in New York called Sigmund Klein's Physical Culture Studio.

The history of bodybuilding, like that of any sport or art, is a history of the men who have bent and shaped it, and Sig Klein is one of them—one of the classiest. Two years ago in New York, just after he retired, he told me how he thought modern bodybuilding began, and it turned out to be a story about another one—a strongman who became the world's first physique artist:

"People say, 'Well, when did systematic bodybuilding start?'
Well, the ancient Greeks had it. The ancient Chinese had it. But how

it came to the so-called civilized world—if you want to call it that, which it isn't—is another story. I believe that it got its first big push in Prussia in 1811, at a time when the Prussians had been defeated by Napoleon and were not allowed to arm their men anymore for battle. There was a man then by the name of Friedrich Ludwig Jahn who was a strict nationalist, and he said he was going to train men in physical culture to be able to defend themselves. Now, there were a lot of men that may not have been strong enough to do gymnastics, so he evolved this system of bodybuilding exercises with the weights. Moderate weights. Now, some of these fellows liked the weights more than they did gymnastics—it could be the truth, it may not be. But let's suppose that a lot of these men began to like the weights better than the gymnastics, and they started little clubs. And this spread all over Germany.

"Now I've got to come back into the story of Attila. Louis Attila was born in Baden-Baden in Germany, in 1844. It's going back quite a long time. He started in the theatrical field as a dance and song man when he was a young man. And in those days they always had professional strongmen in these different vaudeville houses. And then—speculating again—here he meets a man by the name of Felice Napoli. Felice Napoli was born in Naples—that's where he took that professional name, Napoli—in 1820. And he was the finest performer there was of strongmen feats. There were other strongmen, but never with the finesse that he had. Well, Attila wanted to get into the strongman profession, so he became an assistant to Napoli, and he learned the finest art of displaying feats of strength. Then later Attila spread out for himself and he became a very famous performer all over Europe. In 1887, at Queen Victoria's jubilee, of all the strongmen in Europe that could have been selected, they selected him as the strongman to perform at Queen Victoria's jubilee. He was presented by the Prince of Wales with a stickpin the size of a silver dollar, with a crystal painting of a little Hercules statue carved out of crystal, and thirty six big diamonds around there. Later on he had an audience at Buckingham Palace. He had royal families in Denmark taking lessons from him, and he became world famous.

"Now, at this same time there was a strongman act in London by the name of Samson and Cyclops. Samson, Charles Samson, claimed that he was the strongest man in the world, and was constantly challenging everybody to come up on the stage and lift his weights. Attila was upset with this man. He knew him very well and knew that

Frank Zane onstage

Doryphorus by Polycletus (*The Bettmann Archive*)

The *Farnese Hercules* by Glycon of Athens (*The Bettmann Archive*)

Personification of *Day* by Michelangelo
(The Bettmann Archive)

Creation of Adam by Michelangelo
(The Bettmann Archive)

Anatomical Proportions of Man, by Albrecht
Durer (*The Bettmann Archive*)

Muscular Legs, from the notebooks of
Leonardo da Vinci (*The Bettmann Archive*)

ARTICULATE MUSCLE
The Body as Art
A Live Exhibition
by
Arnold Schwarzenegger,
Frank Zane
& Ed Corney

The Whitney Museum of American Art
Madison Avenue at 75th Street

Wednesday
February 25th 1976 at 8 PM

Photographs by George Butler from the forthcoming movie "PUMPING IRON" *he was a braggart. Now, Attila had a school in Brussels and he had some pupils from the Leyden University coming there, taking lessons from him, and one of them was an art student and he said, 'Professor, we have a model in our class that has the finest physique that I've ever seen.'*

"Well, the professor had heard these stories before, and he said, 'Well, if he's as great as you say he is, you bring him to me.' And they brought a young man over to Attila's gymnasium and his name was Frederick Muller. And when Attila asked this young man to strip down, he was shocked and amazed at the beauty of this young man's form. Attila thought, I'm going to train this young man, train him for a couple of years, and accept Samson's challenge.

"Then finally one day Attila says, 'We're ready.' So they get into London and Attila and this young man are in a box when Samson makes his usual every-night challenge and Attila jumps out on the stage and says, 'I challenge you!'

"Samson says, 'You're going to challenge me?'

"He says, 'No. Not me. I'm challenging you for a pupil of mine.' Attila brought the young man up on the stage. He had him dressed in evening clothes. Beautiful blond, curly hair.

"Samson started to laugh. He says, "This young man's going to beat me?'

"Attila says, 'Yes. He is!' Then he had him disrobe and the audience went wild when they saw this beautiful, handsome, magnificent young man.

"He beat Samson, and his name was spread all over London, of course. And then another contest was arranged, and in England they were paying as high as fifty to a hundred dollars for a seat in the theater to see this contest, and the young man beat him again. This young man was the great Sandow, and that was the beginning of his career. Because of him gymnasiums started up, people started to buy dumbbells all over England. And England became the big center of the strongmen. Now the strongmen came over from Europe, over to England, to get into the act. Everybody wanted to make a fortune and they all came to England, all the famous strongmen of Europe. And some of them were much stronger than Sandow, but none of them had the personality, the showmanship, that Attila taught to Sandow.

"All right. Now, there used to be a firm here in New York who were importers of big bands and big acts from Europe. And once they saw Sandow perform they thought, maybe we could bring him to America and make some money.

Poster for live bodybuilding exhibition at Whitney Museum

117

Eugene Sandow, c. 1899

Sandow lifting 19 people and a dog

Louis Cyr's one finger lift

Louis Cyr, c. 1901

121

They convinced Sandow to come to this country, and then when they had him here they didn't know what to do with him. But there was a young man that was getting into show business at the time by the name of Florenz Ziegfeld. The firm contacted him and they sold him Sandow's contract and thought they were glad to be rid of him. This was in 1893, at the Chicago World's Fair. But Ziegfeld had a real showmanship instinct. He took Sandow to Chicago, publicized him as the strongest man in the world, made him more famous than he'd ever been, and all over the country the dumbbells became popular.

"And that was it. That was how bodybuilding really began over here."

In his leotards, mustache and Roman sandals, Eugene Sandow happened to America at a time in Western society when appreciation of the male body was at an all-time low. Since the time of Raphael the male nude had been a distant second to the female as a serious subject of art; Victorianism had covered it from spats to chin, and the Industrial Revolution had devalued it, making

Steve Reeves, 1947

Delacroix drawing from contemporary photographs

123

PETER AISBRENER

SOLOMON PANARES

Do You Own A Car?

I'm not interested in what make it is. But every year you spend a neat little bank roll to keep her in running order. Engine troubles, tire repairs, carbon cleaning, repainting represents quite an expense you readily pay out to keep your car in running condition. And you never dream of giving such care and attention to the human machine—your body. Do you value your car more than your own body? You can't "drive" yourself to the limit all the time, remember. The body can only stand a certain amount of abuse and neglect—then comes the crash! An ounce of prevention is worth a ton of cure. Give your body at least the same thoughtful care you'd give your car. Do it TODAY! If you neglect the old buz-wagon till she's almost ready for the junk pile you pay much more dearly than if you had her fixed right away. So with yourself; don't keep putting off this human overhauling any longer. Don't wait till you're ready to be pushed in a wooden kimona when it's too late. Send your enrollment without another moment's delay.

JOE SANDOW, 1ˢᵗ Prize Winner, 1924

From the collection of Charles Roman

K. V. IYER

E. J. SEVA

Let Me Give You Pierce-Arrow Glands!

Your physical condition depend upon your "insides". There's no sense in developing big, lumpy muscles unless your heart, stomach, lungs, liver, kidneys, nervous and sexual systems are all in perfect condition. They are the real "works". You may have big chunky muscles, but what use are they if not backed up with inner strength, endurance, reserve power, stamina and virility? Get your "engine" properly overhauled by a recognised Master Human Mechanic. Put yourself in my care right away and you won't need any monkey glands. Nor do you require heavy apparatus, springs, dumb-bells or other exercising devices. Science has discovered a better, easier, surer, quicker, more efficient way to stimulate and vitalize all the inner organs and external muscular system. You have everything to gain and nothing to lose. I take all the risk—you take none. Health and strength are here waiting for you, why not accept them now?

CLEVIO MASSIMO, "Muscle Marvel"

Ben Weider "discovering" Reg Park, 1947

Charles Atlas and friend

Early representation of Joe Weider

By permission of Charles Atlas, Ltd., New York, New York

physical strength largely unimportant for the first time in history.

But once here, the redoubtable Sandow, just as he had done in Europe, reminded an entire male generation of what their bodies could look like and do. His physique and strength demonstrations were so popular that at one point he was earning from fifteen hundred to two thousand dollars a week from them, and, as a result of the excitement he created, bodybuilding began to enjoy the closest thing it has ever had to a heyday.

On hand at the time to help was an ex-wrestler and kinesi-therapist named Bernarr "Body Love" Macfadden—the first man to stage an actual physique competition and the first in a line of publisher-promoter-businessman types who have controlled them ever since. In 1898, riding the Sandow boom and the slogan "Weakness is a crime. Don't be a criminal," Macfadden began a magazine called Physical Culture. And in

127

Mr. Canada Contest, 1946

"In the Guise of a Tribesman," Montosh Roy,
Mr. Universe, 1951

"Dark Archer," Montosh Roy

1903, as a promotional device for that magazine, he put on the first physique contest ever at the old Madison Square Garden. Even at the beginning, apparently, it was hard to resist hoking up a bodybuilding competition: at the end of his show Macfadden was arrested for having "a number of toothsome women walking around the stage in their underwear."

At that first contest a physical director named A1 Treloar won a thousand dollars and the title of "the Most Perfectly Developed Man in America." Nineteen years later in the same Garden, the same title was won by a twenty-nine-year-old Calabrian named Angelo Siciliano who called himself Charles Atlas, and bodybuilding took another giant step forward, smack into the tarbaby of big business.

Atlas' course in "Dynamic Tension"—the training theory he devised to get back at that immortal bully who kicked sand in his face one day at Coney Island—has sold seventy thousand copies in seven languages annually since then; and four generations of comic books have carried his ad, showing a muscular-man with a big smile who seems gently amused at the world's flabbiness and asks for only fifteen minutes a day to turn it into muscle. If, as a lot of bodybuilders feel, Atlas and his ad have not had an altogether good effect on bodybuilding, they did at least and for certain introduce it to a broader public than it had had before. And, more centrally to the recent history of the sport, they served as the first irrefutable example that there was money to be made in selling muscles.

For many years Macfadden's annual competition was the only one around, but in the 1930's, with Atlas smiling and selling strongly in the pulps, contests and titles began to sprout all over America. Then in 1939, the American Athletic Union with its usual fondness for order decided to step in and regulate everything by sponsoring state and sectional competitions and a single, ultimately national one. This was the Mr. America contest, won that first year by a man named Roland Essmaker, and it marked the beginning of bodybuilding's ambiguous modern era.

During the forties and fifties—with various kinds of sanctioned and unsanctioned competitions going on all over the country, with different organizations, magazines and barbell companies being created, and with the internecine struggles that all of this new activity produced—the heretofore thin, pure history of bodybuilding becomes Byzantine with complexities that are as boring to write about as they are to hear. The highlights are enough.

Of the competitors there was John Grimek, Mr. America of 1940 and '41, a dignified man, a superb poser, and one of the three or four greatest bodybuilders of all times. And his friend and student, Steve Stanko, who was Mr. America in 1944, and who won the first Mr. Universe title in Philadelphia in 1947. In the late forties and fifties there was Steve Reeves, another Mr. America, who quit bodybuilding after he won the National Amateur British Bodybuilding Association's Mr. Universe title in London to go make Italian Hercules films and become, next to Charles Atlas, the most widely known of all bodybuilders. There were also Reg Park, and Clancey Ross, and Bill Pearl, each of whom was, at his own time, the best there was; and others like George Eifferman, Zabo Koszewski, and Armand Tanny of the old Muscle Beach group, who were good too.

Of the publisher-businessmen who succeeded Bernarr Macfadden as contest sponsors and general promoters of the sport, there were, and still are, three primary ones: Bob Hoffman, a weight-lifting coach and AAU official who publishes two muscle magazines and owns York Barbell Company and a subsidiary that sells health foods and supplements; Joe Weider, a Canadian who lives in California, and whose Weider Enterprises also controls two magazines and a barbell and food-products company; and a former CBS Sealtest Strongman named Dan Lurie, who does roughly the same things in a smaller way and heads a professional bodybuilding organization called the World Body Building Guild.

Tony Sansone, c. 1940

Atlas himself might be amazed at the size of the business these guys do. The domestic and foreign circulation of the Weider magazines, for instance, is over a million; and the yearly advertising budget for only one of Welder's dozens of products, a cable body-shaper, is nearly three million dollars. All of them have become wealthy because of bodybuilding. All of them sell their companies' products through their respective magazines, and all of them use bodybuilders or ex-bodybuilders to advertise those products. Given all of that in common, you would think they'd have a lot to say to each other. But the fact is—and it is a damaging fact to bodybuilding—they don't, and whatever they have to say about each other generally falls into the category of slander.

Of the organizations that followed the AAU into bodybuilding, the most important is the International Federation of Bodybuilders, based in Montreal and run by Joe Welder's brother Ben, who is probably the most selfless of the men now involved in promoting the sport and unquestionably the one who has done the most to advance it. The IFBB is a well-run international organization and the eleventh largest sports federation in the world, with eighty-three member nations, all of which stage physique contests. In addition to it and the AAU in America there is Lurie's WBBG, and in England there is the twenty-five-year-old National Amateur British Bodybuilding Association, or NABBA, a private operation.

John Grimek, 1941

Again, it would seem logical for these organizations to

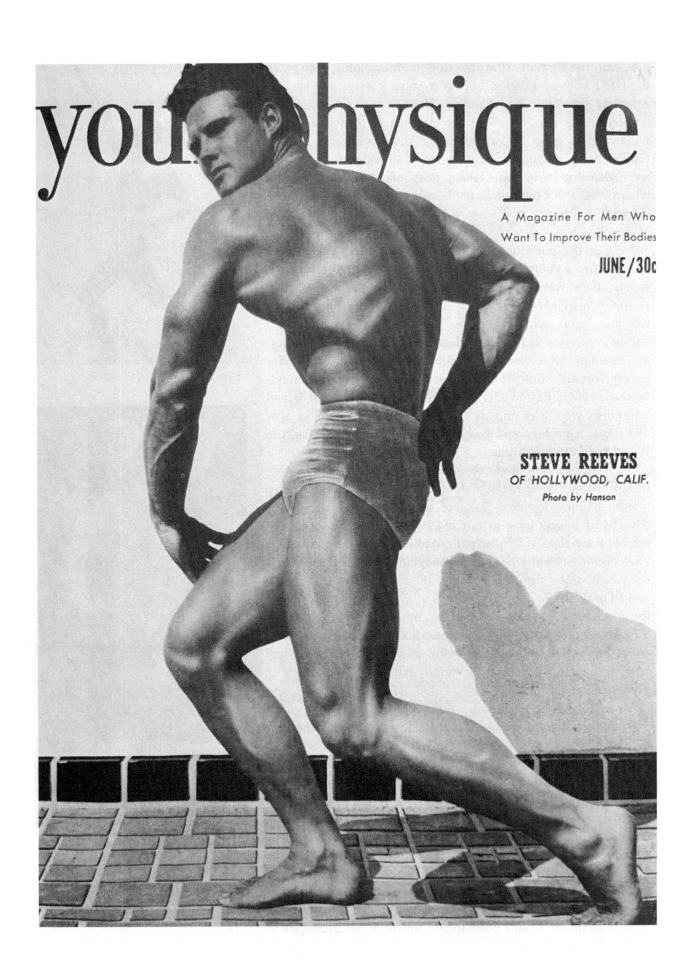

your physique

A Magazine For Men Who
Want To Improve Their Bodies

JUNE/30c

STEVE REEVES
OF HOLLYWOOD, CALIF.
Photo by Hanson

cooperate for the good of the sport. They don't. Each prefers to pretend that the others don't exist. And because of the traditional absence of cooperation and goodwill between them, bodybuilding in this country has stood virtually still in almost every important way since 1950. There are more contests around, a little more cab fare, and arms now are over twenty inches. But the big things, the big things—the shoddy contests and the magazines that reinforce the general public's image of physique competitions as deviant exhibitions in seedy basements full of wine-drunk voyeurs, the insularity that allows all the various myths about bodybuilders to continue, the petty organizational jealousies and resentments that keep them from entering whatever competitions they want to enter, and the nasty fact that despite all the cash around it is still impossible for any but the one or two best builders in the world to make anything like a living at the sport—have stayed the same. And they wouldn't have if some of those organizers and promoters had been doing a little less scratching and hauling for themselves and a little more for the sport.

One thing that has been accomplished since the forties is the creation of a welter of new contests. But because many of these are mutually exclusive, because a number of the titles are identically named, and because the organizations that sponsor them refuse to work together for an overall system of competetion, the results have not been of any great benefit to body-builders. To anyone else the results can seem downright ludi-crous.

Here is a list of the major amateur and professional body building titles given every year and the organizations that award them. There are literally thousands of lesser titles conferred annually in America—state, city and regional titles, titles like Mr. Boiled-Peanut Festival, or Mr. Miracle Mile. These are the big ones.

Dave Draper, Mr. Universe, 1966

Jean-Louis Auger,
Modern Canadian strongman

  AAU: Mr. America, Mr. World, Mr. U.S.A.
  IFBB: Mr. America, Mr. World, Mr. Universe, Mr. Olympia
         (professional).
  WBBG: Mr. America (professional), Mr. World (professional),
         Mr. Galaxy (professional).
  NABBA: Mr. Universe, Mr. Universe (professional).

In 1973, Jimmy Morris of the AAU, Lou Ferrigno of the IFBB, and Chris Dickerson of the WBBG, were all Mr. Americas, Dickerson for the second time, since he had already won the AAU version of that title. Roy Duval, Ken Waller and Boyer Coe were all Mr. Worlds, Coe for the second year in a row and after having also been an AAU Mr. America, and Waller after having been the IFBB Mr. America. Coe, Dickerson and Ferrigno (who had been an

Courtesy of the Weider Brothers

IFBB and a WBBG Mr. America but never an AAU, because they won't let you in if you've been in the other two, any more than the IFBB will if you've been in a WBBG contest before theirs, or in an NABBA either for that matter) were the three Mr. Universes.

All of this, of course, makes perfect sense to a bodybuilder. He knows that some of these titles mean more than others, and which ones have what significance—knows, for instance, that of the amateur titles the IFBB Mr. Universe and the older NABBA one are now the most prestigious, having replaced the AAU Mr. America; and that the Olympia is the top contest of all, that the chances are excellent that whoever holds that title in a given year is the best bodybuilder alive, the true Mr. World, Galaxy arid Universe. But to ordinary people (among them all the fans that bodybuilding presently doesn't have), it appears laughable and meaningless to have so many puffy, interchangeable-sounding designations floating around, and to have so little, well, hierarchy or something to the whole thing.

And so it is. But a meaningful and sensible titular structure, like a number of other things bodybuilding needs, could result only from all those acronymic groups living together, and for the present they are not willing to do that. Besides, none of them has ever worried too much about what the ordinary people think anyway.

Few things are more fascinating or moving to human beings than bodies. We all have one and covet others; we look to them for pleasure and gratification, for sensory information, for protection and flight and communication. We stare at them, fondle them, make love to and with them, develop fetishes about them, indulge them, ponder them. And at some point we all, every mother's son or daughter of us, care about how ours looks. Furthermore, most of us care in a cheerfully Platonic way—granting, every time we notice that we are too fat or have good calves, the existence somewhere of an ideal waistline, an ideal calf.

Given the fascination and the inclination to idealize, it should be perfectly natural for people to find interest in bodies that have been developed and worked as far as the medium of flesh will allow—that are not only bodies but symbols, every bit as universal and articulate as carved marble or bronze, of our physical potential and limitation. It should be, and in Asia, the Middle East and parts of Europe, places where bodybuilding is vastly more popular than it is here, it seems to be very natural indeed. Perhaps it would be in America too, where almost all the best bodybuilders are, if it were not for the fact that body building over here has seemed determined to keep itself a secret. Ever since Sandow hung up his leotards, the internals of the sport seem almost to have conspired to keep this one, simple truth from

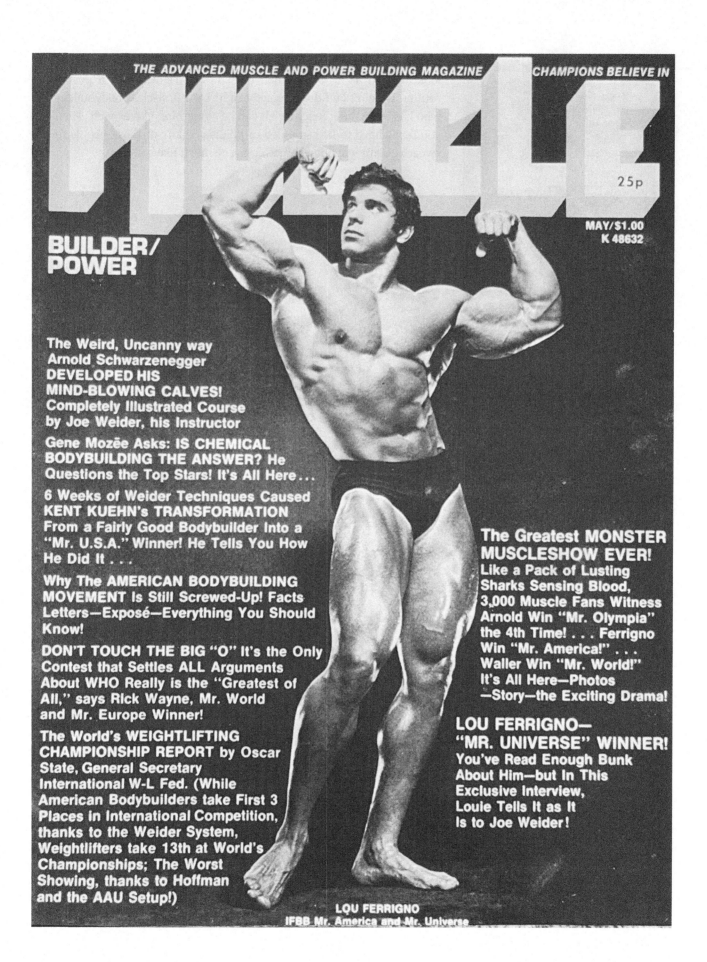

THE ADVANCED MUSCLE AND POWER BUILDING MAGAZINE   CHAMPIONS BELIEVE IN

MUSCLE

25p

BUILDER/
POWER

MAY/$1.00
K 48632

The Weird, Uncanny way
Arnold Schwarzenegger
DEVELOPED HIS
MIND-BLOWING CALVES!
Completely Illustrated Course
by Joe Weider, his Instructor

Gene Mozëe Asks: IS CHEMICAL
BODYBUILDING THE ANSWER? He
Questions the Top Stars! It's All Here...

6 Weeks of Weider Techniques Caused
KENT KUEHN's TRANSFORMATION
From a Fairly Good Bodybuilder Into a
"Mr. U.S.A." Winner! He Tells You How
He Did It...

Why The AMERICAN BODYBUILDING
MOVEMENT Is Still Screwed-Up! Facts
Letters—Exposé—Everything You Should
Know!

DON'T TOUCH THE BIG "O" It's the Only
Contest that Settles ALL Arguments
About WHO Really is the "Greatest of
All," says Rick Wayne, Mr. World
and Mr. Europe Winner!

The World's WEIGHTLIFTING
CHAMPIONSHIP REPORT by Oscar
State, General Secretary
International W-L Fed. (While
American Bodybuilders take First 3
Places in International Competition,
thanks to the Weider System,
Weightlifters take 13th at World's
Championships; The Worst
Showing, thanks to Hoffman
and the AAU Setup!)

The Greatest MONSTER
MUSCLESHOW EVER!
Like a Pack of Lusting
Sharks Sensing Blood,
3,000 Muscle Fans Witness
Arnold Win "Mr. Olympia"
the 4th Time! . . . Ferrigno
Win "Mr. America!" . . .
Waller Win "Mr. World!"
It's All Here—Photos
—Story—the Exciting Drama!

LOU FERRIGNO—
"MR. UNIVERSE" WINNER!
You've Read Enough Bunk
About Him—but In This
Exclusive Interview,
Louie Tells It as It
Is to Joe Weider!

LOU FERRIGNO
IFBB Mr. America and Mr. Universe

Joe Weider at work

Ben Weider: President, IFBB

getting out: for whatever reasons, a physique competition is *fun* to look at. And at its best—when the show is right, when a posing routine is being laid down exactly right by a first-class bodybuilder who has everything together—it can be something else as well. Then you don't have to be reminded of Phidias or any of those people to swear you are watching something very much like art.

Franco Columbu

134

Eight
Mr. Olympia No. 3

There is no question on which side are the two thousand people swelling the Brooklyn Academy of Music for the 1973 IFBB Mr. America, Mr. World and Mr. Olympia contests. From the Miss Americana contestants backstage, fighting over pens with which to give away their addresses, to the iridescent fags glimmering quietly in the great dim lobby, this one four-thousandth of New York knows exactly how to look. Expert, persnickety, rabid—these people are fans.

They have been here now for three hours, watching speeches, presentations, balancing acts, and over fifty amateur bodybuilders in the first two contests. They have just witnessed the strange and determined expiration on stage of Serge Nubret. They are ready to be plied.

The cheering starts before Martin Stader can finish the introduction, and it continues through the full two minutes that Franco Columbu allows the empty stage and the audience to wait for him. Franco wants them ductile when he comes out. He has listened to Nubret's applause, knows he died, and is not sur prised. He and Arnold Schwarzenegger put it to the Lion a little bit backstage, not pumping up while he did, walking around in shorts to show Nubret what Gold's Gym legs are like. Little things, to help him psych himself. Franco didn't know it then, but it wasn't really necessary. Nubret had already had all the psyching he needed.

An hour before the prejudging that afternoon there was already a crowd clustered around the back door of the Academy. It was a colorful mixture of Lafayette Square dudes, photographers, fidgety

"When I'm on the stage I control everybody down there in the audience. I'm very secure about myself, and I think I am much higher than anybody there because I'm on the stage doing the work. And they are watching me. They paid to see me. And I'm very confident. Very, very confident. And I, I show much possibility. I'm not afraid of anything. I am very secure."
—Franco Columbu

Serge Nubret arriving,
Brooklyn Academy of Music

tight-skirted groupies, and an assortment of bodybuilders who lounged against the building and on the customized cars, arms folded on their chests, eyeing each other lazily. And suddenly there was Serge Nubret, big as a house, getting out of a limousine with his glamorous wife, Jacqueline, and his manager, a chubby Spanish cosmetics executive named Paco. Now, you talk about *class*—a rich foreign manager with a briefcase, a limo, and a dynamite wife in a sherbet-green blouse! The crowd stiffened appreciatively, milled, angling for looks. Nubret sidled into it, followed by his wife and manager. He gave out a couple of obligatory handshakes and stood for a moment on the sidewalk talking remotely, his hands crossed at his crotch, his dark face somber, like Senator Hugh Scott holding a news conference— looking, well, a little *embarrassed* by all this and more than a little put out. Then with Jacqueline on his arm he made his way abruptly into the Academy, leaving a definite and lingering impression of downright uppityness out on the street.

But it wasn't arrogance Nubret was showing the people out there. To understand what it was, as well as what happened to his posing routine later that evening, you would have had to see him the afternoon before in Tom Minichiello's gym, where he ran into a photographer with pictures of the competition. Nubret had come in friendly and relaxed for a protein drink or two and some conversation with the boys in the gym. Jaqueline perched herself eloquently on a couch. Paco began showing pictures of naked women. Dressed in black, Serge had stood in the middle of the lobby and thumbed through some recent photographs of Franco and Arnold—his right hand shaking noticeably, everything going bleak on him all at once.

When Franco does come out it is right now. In a hop he is on the posing dais, thick as a howitzer shell, hitting shot after shot. *Bap, bap, bap.* Franco's routine is like a speedbag workout— quick and ferocious, with a loud, fast rhythm. He gets off twice as many poses as Nubret, without hurry and without missing a move, coming off the line of one with sharp, precise motions that stab into the next: squat, thick, dramatic poses that don't try for length or flow but make the most of his overall development and the magnificent depth and clarity of his muscles. A chant begins in the audience and grows: "Franco, Franco, Franco. . ."

Bap, bap, bap, bap, bap goes the best short man in the business. And when he leaves he is close to tears.

"I was thinking when I got out there on the stage to pull the people into me and make them happy. I went out very slow and I was very, very happy with the applause. When I was going back to the dressing room, I felt inside very close to the audience, I almost cried."

"I wasn't thinking about any-thing or anybody in particular. I was thinking about all of them. What I was really thinking in the moments when I was doing one pose and they applause so much, and my mind was really with the next pose, thinking gonna be more, gonna hit even harder and the next one more hard, till it was so convincing that they would scream more and more and more till they couldn't take it anymore."
—Franco Columbu

Nine

Joe Disco took me to my first physique contest. It was held at the big, gaunt downtown YMCA in Birmingham. It was an AAU contest, maybe a Mr. Alabama, and there had been a powerlifting competition before it. I remember that the room was badly lighted and smelled of liniment and sweat. It had been kept cool for the lifters, and there was a lot of white dust on the floor from the chalk they use on their hands.

Disco said to pick out a particular good guy and watch what he did, not to try to flock-watch the whole bunch, because then I'd miss the point of what was going on. But I wasn't able to do that, and the main thing I remember is being visually confused by the amount of staring flesh out there on that white floor, and though I had seen plenty of guys pose before in front of the mirrors at Magic City, a little embarrassed by it too—by the way some of their feet were white with chalk, and how bare the room was, and how a few of them had goose bumps from the cold. Afterward I wasn't sure what to say to Disco, or even how to feel. I've been with a good many people at their first body contests since then, and very few of them can put a finger on what they feel after seeing real posing for the first time. One who could is a lady in New York named Virginia, and I'll tell about her a little later.

A lot of contests are held in YMCA's, though they are hardly ever good places to hold them. Most AAU physique competitions, including the Mr. America, are still pinned to the tails of powerlifting meets and they, particularly, tend to be held in Y's, boys' clubs, Electricians' Halls and high-school gyms—vacant, stage-less places

"I wouldn't want a woman that would have mauled me because of my physique, or was a sex maniac who just was a body freak, a body queen, who was just interested in rubbing suntan lotion on me and getting all hot and bothered every time she looked at me. You know, my wife is interested in personality, is interested in the real humanness of a person. We don't sit there with her admiring my physique, you know, and drooling and waiting to get to bed with me."
—Mike Katz

Mr. and Mrs. Bob Klez

141

Pumping up

with bad lighting that are much more suitable to lifting than to bodybuilding.

Contests held outdoors, like the WBBG Mr. Fire Island (at which the competition is always less interesting to watch than the crowd it draws), can be fun to go to, but the flat light outside is no good for posing. In its wisdom, the WBBG has put on other shows in places like the Heisman Trophy Room in New York and the Fontainebleau Hotel in Miami Beach, and at those places it is more than just the light that is wrong.

All you really need to put on a physique contest are a deep proscenium stage, good lights and someone who knows how to work them. But all the best places have something else too. It is a quality, similar to the one that distinguishes the best bodybuilding gyms, that makes you feel while you are in one of them that physique competition is the best and most appropriate thing that could possibly happen there. The Academy of Music in Brooklyn is one place like that. Another one is the Pavillion at Mountain Park Amusement Center.

It would be hard to find a better or more symbolic place to see your first bodybuilding show than Mountain Park—which is a loud, raunchy, vibrating little island of gaudery surrounded by the clipped lawns of suburban Holyoke. It would be a Sunday in the summer or fall when you'd be there, and you might be there for the Junior Mr. America, or the Mr. East Coast—either one would be fine, because Ed Jubinville runs them both. Outside the Pavillion the roller coaster would be banging up and down its huge wooden trestle, kids would be yelling and there would be a lot of very colorful-looking people doing what they call "struttin' the booths." They dress up for Mountain Park on a Sunday.

By one-thirty the Pavillion would already be more than half filled. That would be a good time to go to the clam bar at the rear of the beamed, barnlike auditorium, get a beer in a Dixie Cup, find a seat up near the front and watch the people coming in. It's a flashy, noisy, animated crowd at the Pavillion, and most of them, even the women, you'd notice, are big—maybe in the same vicarious way that a lot of hockey fans are mean. By two there would be twelve hundred of them, packed shoulder to beefy shoulder in the connected wooden chairs, yelling to each other, sweating, chewing gum and watching the bodybuilders lounge in up near the judges' table (some of them carrying little bags with trunks and oil and a towel in them, and almost all of them *dressed*, Jack— a few, like Tony Roma or Tony Carroll, in clothes they design themselves); watching as they move on up to the stage and shake hands with Ed, and as they sign in and are measured for their height class; studying every move the builders make even though they might be talking to you at the same time, because they are fans and that's what they

Oiling up

Tall Class, Mountain Park

Ray Delaney in a single biceps

Franklin Green

*"Winning Mr. America is a tre-
mendous responsibility. Even
having muscles is a tremendous
responsibility. People look up to
you. They think you're some sort
of a special person, and you always have to seem to feel that
way too whether you do or not.
You start looking at people,
whether they're inferior to you
maybe no other way but physically, that no matter how they
treat you or feel about you, you
always have the muscles there."*
—Steve Michalik

Pose-Off

are here for, to watch, and also because to them, the small-time
builders and hardhats and housewives and factory workers that
are bodybuilding fans here and everywhere, these builders are
magical—aristocratic and significant as the Dolphins in their
locker room—and because watching them, just watching them
move around up there, is . . . exciting, is what it is.

"That's Gordon Babb," one of them might tell you. "Best
Back, Mr. A. And there's Franklin Green over there, the one with
all the rings. Franklin's outtasight. Hey, Franklin, baby. You gotta
see this guy to believe him—the *abs*, the *serratus* . . ."

He would probably point out Ray Delaney to you, and Bob
Klez, and Martin Joyce, and tell you about Joyce's 720-pound
deadlift. And for sure he would point out Leon Brown, who is often
a winner at Mountain Park and always a favorite. Last summer at
the Pavillion just before a contest that the crowd had Leon picked
to win, the word got around that big Lou Ferrigno was there and
going to enter. Lou was bulking up then for the Mr. America in the
fall, and he was carrying around 280 pounds. The crowd watched
noncommittally as he hulked up to the sign-in table to give his
name, and then as he walked over to the leopard-skin posing dais
and began stomping on it to test it for his weight. "No class," said
a guy sitting next to me, watching Louie stomp. "The kid's just got
no class." Later on, when another word came around that Lou had
changed his mind about entering because Jubinville wouldn't pay
him anything and because Leon looked too cut up, the guy turned
to me again and grinned, his day made. "You see what I mean?"
he said. "Class tells."

Over to the left of where you would be sitting is "the
pit," the place the competitors go after they are measured, to
change into their posing trunks, to oil themselves and to pump
up. One nice thing about the Pavillion is that the pit is right out
there with the audience and not backstage as it usually is. Here
it is just a rectangular area made along one wall of the
auditorium by hanging a canvas screen. The screen doesn't go
all the way to the floor or the ceiling, so you can watch the
bodybuilders' feet at the bottom, and dumbbells rising and
falling at the top, and hear them shuffling and muttering behind
it like cattle in a boxcar.

Jubinville likes to start his shows with a few preliminaries,
saving the bodybuilding till last, not tacking it on like an after-
thought the way they do in the AAU—just holding it back and
setting you up. There might be a wrist-wrestling contest, or a
benchpress-deadlift competition. And Ed would probably do his
muscle-control act. Whatever it was, it would be well-managed
and entertaining. And as you sat there with your beer watching
It and listening to the crowd, with the bodybuilders off in the
pit to your left getting ready, you still wouldn't know what to

Pose-off, Delaney and Klez

expect of a physique contest, but you would know without doubt that you were in the right place to see one, whatever it was.

George Butler and Virginia and I got to the Brooklyn Academy of Music about an hour before the prejudging was due to start. There was already a good crowd out back around the stage door, talking and enjoying the hot September sun. A lot of the New York bodybuilders were there, and a few of the ones from California, and some people we hadn't seen since Baghdad: Winston Roberts was there from Canada, and Mike Katz. Everybody was having a fine time, standing around in the sun and seeing people they hadn't seen since the last big show.

Arnold arriving
Brooklyn Academy of Music

I introduced Virginia to Mike. He was leaning on a car with his big arms crossed on his chest, dressed quietly as he always is, in a way that mutes his size and proportions. He shook her hand and grinned down at her in a pleased, gentle way, as though he had been hoping just that morning to meet her. A few minutes later he asked me if that was my wife.

"No. An old friend from Alabama now living in New York."

"Some old friend. She's dynamite."

"She wants to know about bodybuilding. But she can't come tonight, so she wanted to see the prejudging."

"The prejudging definitely wants to see her, too."

There was a nice breeze blowing, and the sky was very blue for New York. Leon Brown arrived. And then Kent Kuehn and Denny Cable and some of the others from Gold's. Serge Nubret pulled up in a limousine with his wife and manager, and did not dawdle on the street. After a while the man at the stage door who checks the passes said they were about to get it going upstairs, and almost everyone moved in, leaving the sun and a few girl friends and groupies and kids outside.

"Everybody here seems to know everybody else," Virginia said as I followed her in through the metal doors. "It's like a kind of party. And everybody's so . . . sweet."

She went to college at Sweet Briar, or Randolph-Macon, one of those schools in the state of Virginia that used to specialize in debutantes, which she was—and particularly in lovely ones from good Southern backgrounds, which she also was. Now, after six or seven years in New York, she was still unmarried, still had that musical variation of the Southern accent that belongs like a facial feature to a certain class of women down there and that gives each word a deep whiskey color, and still walked and tossed her head as though she were doing those things on a country-club tennis court early in the morning. Mike Katz was not the only person around who enjoyed looking at her. People had been doing that all her life, and if the looking made some of them ignore or forget how smart she was, that had never been Virginia's fault.

Arnold

153

We took the elevator up to the auditorium level in a crowd of bodybuilders and contest officials and walked with them down the long concrete corridor, past the pit room where the Mr. America competitors were getting ready, to the stage. Tommy Minichiello, who runs the America-World-Olympia show when it is held in New York, was trying to get the judges together at a table and adjust some big klieg lights at the same time. Behind him on the stage a lot of people were milling around—bodybuilders, and photographers, and a few of the Miss Americana contestants, already in their bikinis and stiletto pumps. Virginia and George and I went out into the big, nearly deserted auditorium and sat in the fifth row. Virginia crossed her legs and settled into the seat as naturally as if she were there to hear Richebourg Gaillard McWilliams speak on the history of Mobile.

"Now, Chawes," she said, looking through her purse for something, "I want to know about *everything* that happens."

A prejudging in bodybuilding is the contest. What is called the contest is really a show whose results have already been determined the morning or afternoon before by the prejudging. Prejudgings are held only for the big competitions, and though they lack some of the drama and the crowd reactions of the contests, they are often more interesting to watch, and they will always teach you more about bodybuilding. In that way they are rather like the school-figure part of skating competitions—the technical, straight-faced part where the nature of the competition is more apparent, where it is easiest to determine what exactly is being judged and how.

In all IFBB contests except the Olympia, which has no divisions, a prejudging begins by dividing the contestants into three height classes: the short men, who are less than five feet five; the mediums, between five five and five eight; and the tall men, who are over five eight. Depending on the contest, from three to six places are awarded within each height category, and the overall title winner is chosen from the three class winners. In most competitions there are also awards given for best individual body parts—best arms, legs, chest, back and abdominals—as well as a best-poser trophy. All of this makes for a lot of evaluating, and in a show like the America-World-Olympia, where over fifty bodybuilders have to be looked at in a space of three hours or less, the prejudging has got to be very well organized from the beginning.

The judges (there are always either five or seven) do their judging in three rounds from a table placed about twenty feet from where the builders stand. They judge the short class first, then the mediums and talls, and finally a pose-down between the three class winners for the overall title.

Round one for each height category is a nonscoring preliminary assessment round where the competitors simply parade

Backstage

154

*"If another man can do it, so can
I. And I'm going to do it. I don't
care how much work it takes.
Work doesn't bother me. She
knows. I work hard—I go through
pain, unbelievable suffering,
and I love every minute of it.
Not because you like it—you
don't enjoy it, but somehow you
want to feel that pain in order
to know that you're having a
good workout. Believe me it's
hard work. I don't think there's
any sport in the world, anything
in the world, that takes so much
pain and so much struggle and so
much motivation. And the man
that can stand this can achieve
the top."*
—Tony Roma

"I've had phone calls, letters and personal approaches. How they got my number I'll never know. But they want you, they're going to get you. And I had phone calls and phone calls from people, and maybe I'm stupid because I would not act offended towards these people, because I felt they are human beings as well as I am, and I will just explain to them: "Well this isn't my bag. If you're interested in developing your body I will help you, but as far as anything else goes, I'm not interested.' But maybe the word got around that I was a softie. You know, who knows? So then I got calls and calls, and the letters came. 'Steve, send me photographs of you in leather pants.' 'Steve, send me photographs of you with nothing on; I'll pay any price. I'll pay any price. I'll pay anything.' If I wasn't married and I was homosexual, I could be living for nothing. Putting my entire salary away. I could have any car I want. I could be living in . . . I've had offers to live in Maine. I've had offers to live on Fire Island. I've had offers to live in people's apartments on 86th Street down here, which is a fantastic neighborhood."
—Steve Michalik

in front of the judges, who use the first of seven worksheets to make notes about them. In round two the height class again comes out as a group and stands without flexing or posing, giving the judges front, side and back views as they are requested. The judges are free here to isolate any number of builders at a time for comparisons—asking, maybe, to see "seven and four from the side again," or "numbers one, eight and six men from the back." They are looking in this round less for muscularity than for proportion, symmetry and general appearance, and each judge scores each competitor from 1 to 20 according to what he finds. In the third and final round, the builders come out one by one and each is given ninety seconds to perform a posing routine made up of both compulsory and optional poses. He must start with the compulsory poses. There are six of these: a double-biceps from the front with the abdominals flexed, a front lat spread with flexed legs, a right side-biceps and shoulder with the side of the leg flexed, a back double-biceps, a lat spread from the rear with both calves flexed, and a left side shot with triceps, chest and the left leg flexed. They are the purest poses in bodybuilding. On no one of them is it possible to cheat, and taken as a group they represent each muscle area fairly. The optional poses are in there so that a contestant can individualize, showing the judges his posing style and concentrating on the parts of himself he thinks are the best. A man with good abs, for instance, would do most frontal shots during his optional time, laying a lot of stomach on the judges. This round is scored as the second one was, and when the totals are added and all the height-class places established, the three winners—a short, a medium and a tall—are brought out again to do identical poses side by side until an overall contest winner is decided upon.

This last part is called a pose-off. It lasts for one minute. It is the minute that bodybuilders train all year for, and if all three class winners are good it is a minute you would not forget watching.

"Why do they walk like that?" Virginia wanted to know. She was smoking a menthol cigarette. We were standing at the very back of the auditorium while she did it, looking down an aisle to the stage where the Mr. America short class was parading for the judges. There were maybe a dozen people scattered through the old, frayed Victorian hall—girl friends and wives, and three fast-talking Brooklyn fans who had managed to get passes—but the place felt comfortably vacant and intimate, and exactly right for what was going on. "They do it the same way outside."

"Because they're showing themselves off. Outside and inside, but particularly now. They're showing off the result of all that work I was telling you about, so they strut with it, put it all out front. Their arms ride out like that because of the lats. You remember what the lats are?"

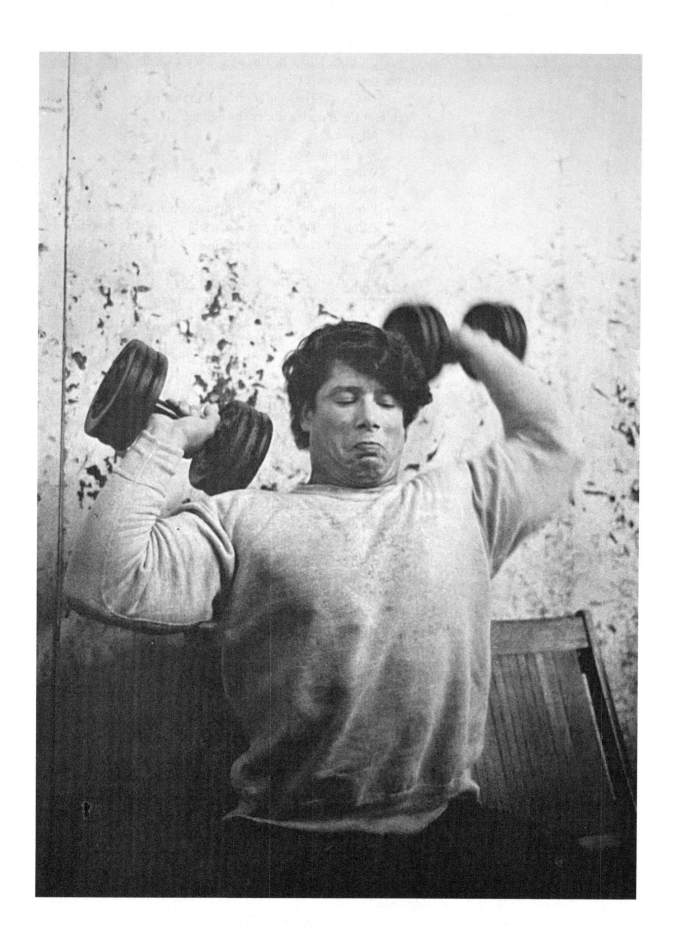

"Uh huh. I *like* it, Chawes. They look like show horses. Why *are* they all sweaty?"

"That's oil. They put it on back in that room we went past, to highlight the muscles under the lights."

"All over?"

"Mostly all over."

"What else?"

"What else what?"

"What else do they do to themselves in there, dummy?"

"Pump up. Do exercises to get blood into the muscles, to make them bigger and bring them out."

"Is that fair?"

"Sure it's fair—that's the point. But it works better for some than for others. There's a great bodybuilder from Chicago named Sergio Oliva who used to win the Olympia every year before Arnold. They say he gets smooth the first time he pumps up, at the prejudging. At night when he pumps up again for the contest all his water is gone from sweating and he looks cut up, but by then he might have already lost. Arnold says that's the way he beat him last year in Germany."

"All his water?"

"That's sort of complicated and not very interesting. A lot of psyching goes on in there, too. All these guys know each other. They meet at the same big contests every year and it's sort of like a convention. All year they're at their own gyms, and then once or twice a year they get together. They have a lot of fun in there, but there's also a lot of staring and checking out. And psyching."

"Like what?"

"Well, like say a guy is coming in this year with bigger arms and he's proud of them. Another guy might come up to him in the pit and say something like "Hey, man, you're looking great, great. But, hey, you sure better work on those arms." It throws him off, and that can hurt his routine. Another thing is the best ones never take off their robes or sweat clothes until the very last. Schwarzenegger sometimes won't pump up at all. He'll just hang around and watch like he doesn't need it, and that screws everybody up."

Virginia giggled. "That's awful. How about this shaving business? Didn't you say they shave all over?"

"Yeah, they do that too. If they didn't you couldn't see the muscles clearly."

"Uh huh." She put out her cigarette with a quick little stab. "Now tell me something else. Are they, uh . . . most of them, do they like girls?"

"All the ones I know. I've heard about some who don't. And there are a few around who play gay for money. But none of the big ones."

"It just seems so—at first, I mean."

"You see your deltoids and you've got things in there, and you could stick who knows what in there and it would get lost. That's muscularity. And the thigh cuts— take a look at Leon [Brown]; Leon could get his fingernails lost in the cuts of his legs. Now that's real muscularity . . . if you get that, there aren't going to be many people around who are going to beat you."
—Mike Katz

The Walk

"People think that who don't know about it. There are plenty of homosexuals who hang around the sport, in the gyms and at the contests. But most of them don't bother anybody, and the bodybuilders don't mind them. Then there are some others with money who get into managing."

"It would just be such a waste."

"What would?"

"If they didn't like girls. Like that one on the left." She pointed to one of the shorts who had been called out of the line with two others. The prejudging was into round two. The three stood without flexing, facing the judges' table. "He is gorgeous. What do you think would happen if I took him back to Alabama? I could take him out to the pool at the club and show him off."

"He might not like the club. But I know he'd like you."

Virginia tossed her head, smiled. "You're right," she said. "He might not like the club."

According to the rules, competitors may "not wear footwear, watches, bangles, pendants or earrings"—or anything else, for that matter, but a brief pair of posing trunks. So they come on stage like that, nervous at first, grabbing looks at the other men, and commence to show the judges their most fundamental selves. Very few smile naturally as they do this. It is supposed to be good to smile while you are posing, so most of them learn to do it, but the smiles always look studied, the way Richard Nixon's do during television speeches. And the judges look at them. Through two scoring rounds they study the bodies relaxed and posed, flexed and unflexed, and write down numbers between one and twenty to indicate what they think of them. That is the form of the competition. The essence of it is in what the judges look for, and how they assess it.

They look first for symmetry and proportion, an overall harmony of parts, the ideal notion of which hasn't changed much since the Greek sculptors; the body should still be seven and a half times the length of the head; the diameters of the neck, upper arms and calves should still be within an inch or two of each other. They also look initially for things like skin tone, posture and skeletal structure. They look at the overall size and shape and relationships of the various muscle groups, and then they look, very carefully and individually, at each one. Starting at the top of the body, they examine the neck and sometimes even the muscles of the face—Reeves and Sandow were both admired for their square, muscular jaws. Around the shoulder area they look for slope and width in the trapezius muscles, and for the two thick pillars that should be apparent where they insert into the back of the head; for density and striation in each of the deltoids and a clear balanced separation of its three sheaths. In the chest they notice how the pectoralis merges with the anterior deltoids, how squarely formed they are and how distinct are the

Prejudging

upper and lower sternum grooves that separate the muscle. When the arms are flexed there should be sharp divisions between the two heads of the biceps and the three of the triceps; they look for that, and for peak to the biceps and a horseshoe declivity at the back of each arm. They look for the iliac furrow and the linea alba in the stomach, and for the segmented carapace of muscle there that is shaped, when it is right, sort of like the shell of a turtle. They check out the obliques, and the serratus—the small knobs of muscle like chunks of rope that tie the rib cage to the lats. The back should be broad and thick, and should taper in a deep curve to the waist down the outer edges of the latissimus dorsi; and when it is flexed, the trapezius, deltoids, teres, infraspinatus and erector muscles should tighten and spring up cleanly under the skin. In the legs they want to see deep furrows between the quadriceps of the frontal thighs, and to be able to see the peroneus longus and sartorius swells, and a sort of cleft-diamond shape to the muscles of the calf.

They look at the forearms, the Achilles tendons, even the feet. Finally they look at how close all the muscles are to the skin, how striated they are and how much adipose tissue there is to blunt them. And when they are done, if they are patient and skillful at what they are doing, each competitor knows what he wants to know: that whatever he has made of himself and brought to the stage has been carefully, thoroughly seen.

Rapt, hardly moving, Virginia sat in the middle of the fifth row and watched everything that happened on the stage from the posing round of the Mr. America through the end of prejudging for the Mr. World. I wanted there to be some good stuff for her to see, and there was. In the America there was Leon Brown with his perfectly chiseled, wasp-waisted build, and his quiet polished routine; and Bob Birdsong, one of the men from Gold's, with a routine he didn't seem to understand, but looking very ripped and close to the skin; and mammoth Louie Ferrigno, who ultimately beat out the other two for the title by outsizing if not out-fitnessing them. In the World there was Ken Waller and Bill Grant in the tall class, and Ed Corney in the medium. From Waller and Kent Kuehn and Jeff Smith and Bill Howard she saw a lot of the flashy, fun-to-watch Gold's Gym posing, a style of wide-open shots and sweeping transitions and dramatic, down-on-one knee flourishes.

Sitting a couple of rows behind us were the three Brooklyn fans, one of them a lumpy teen-ager named Raol who never misses a prejudging in New York and who knows as much about posing as any judge does. During most of the World, Raol pelted the backs of our heads with his quick loud chatter—"That's a Draper pose . . . a Scott three-quarter back. . . . Now watch this. . . . *Awright, awright*, a Sergio double-bicep. . . . Now he'll bring it into a crab . . . Cinch it in, cinchthatmother*in*.

Jimmy Morris

. . . The guy's calves are so bad in front he oughtta stay more to the sides, show the *sides*, turkey. . . ."

Then after the World the judges called a break. The prejudging had been going on for nearly two hours. After the break they would prejudge Serge Nubret, Franco and Arnold for the Mr. Olympia title. Then they would break again, for two or three hours this time, before the show began at eight o'clock. That night the Academy would be aisle-full of Raols—whistlers, screamers, moaners and booers, a nitroglycerin Academy crowd that can chill or frenzy on a second. Each competitor then would have a minute or two before them under the spot on the posing dais. The very best ones and the local favorites like Franklin Green would be met there and followed through their routines by an unimaginable din, an urgent, rhythmic pandemonium that would break some of them into sweaty, glazed-eyed transports on the dais and bring others close to tears. And a few, the inexplicable and ridiculous few who shouldn't be there in the first place but always are—the ones with no muscle, and the ones who can't pose, and the ones who come out with erections—would leave the dais feeling sorry they were in Brooklyn that evening.

Right now, except for some talking on the stage, the place was quiet. Virginia and I walked to the back again for her to smoke.

"Do they tell who won?"

"Not until tonight after the show. Nobody but the judges knows until then. But it looks like Ferrigno in the America and Ken Waller in the World. What did you think?"

"I'd like it better if there weren't so many of them."

"So would I."

"Like maybe five in each height thing, and just the best ones. The ones who aren't so good kind of . . . blur the good ones or something."

"I know. They ought to screen for the big contests, but they don't. It's one of the things they have to improve on. There are some others too."

"But, Jesus God, the posing, Chawes. That Leon guy is . . . IS fantastic. And the ones from that place in California. And your friend, Corney—did you see me when he got through? I couldn't blink my eyes. It was like they were frozen open. His hands and everything, and the way he moves."

He's just had a bad knee operation. He wasn't in the shape he usually is."

"It's like ballet, isn't it? The best ones, I mean."

"Sort of, but you haven't seen the best ones yet. Ed usually is, but he wasn't this time."

"You know what it reminded me of? Of Elizabethan music. No, really; a whole lot. I kept thinking of it while I was watching.

Leon Brown, putting it together

"There's something in any man that wants to be above the average. A bodybuilder is actually the most in perfection of the human body. You want to reach the perfection. To be that sets you apart from the average man—it sets you apart. You are looked up to and respected. I think we do it because . . . it takes a lot of courage, and we dare step out of the regular routine. Not many people dare. . . . We really go down to the limit, and that sets you apart. We go through all this struggle and all this pain, you know, and this is what makes me proud. I can do other things in life much easier."
—Tony Roma

Elliot Gilchrist, fifty-four years old

You know those songs, how they're raunchy and elegant and massive and delicate and surprising all at the same time? And . . . sweet? Stop it. That's just what Corney made me think of, and a few of the others. And also of horses—Tennessee walking horses I used to see at shows in Winchester."

"I'm glad you liked it."

"Their thighs look like horses. Do you have thighs like that?"

"No. Look, are you getting tired?"

"They even look like they eat alfalfa and clover. And the way they move."

"Virginia?"

"What?"

"You'd better find something to hang on to for these last three."

"I haven't seen anything, huh?"

"You've seen something. But there's a lot you haven't seen."

Ken Waller, Mr. World, 1973

Ten
Mr. Universe No. 3

And crazy is what they went, exactly—all three thousand or so people inside and outside the Al-Nasr Cinema, as soon as the Mr. Universe winner's hand was lifted by Ben Weider. Crazier than crazy. The place simply imploded toward that single spot, the dais on which he stood, and from there it must have looked to him and the others on the stage like a stained tidal wave of open mouths and frantic extremities crashing at them. What they did about it was make tracks for the dressing room.

There was supposed to be protection there, a dozen badged and billied officials whose job it was to get the winners reasonably back to their hotels. But all the officials in Baghdad would have been as powerless as those were before the mad, rioting crush of hero-hungry Arabs that filled the halls and dressing rooms as suddenly as if they had been vacuumed there from the auditorium. Iraqi officials are used to hopelessness. They gave out a few desultory whacks to anyone within range and just let it go at that. And Mike Katz and Ed Corney, both half-dressed and carrying huge brass trophies, were digested by the crowd in separate lumps and swept from the building into the street before they even knew that there was no order to this thing, no *plan*.

There was a jam outside the Cinema, and Corney and I looked around, momentarily not being moved, each clutching an end of one of the three-foot trophies Ed had won, like a log in open water, and saw over the heads of thousands of Arabs thousands more, in the streets, standing on top of cars—a Darryl F. Zanuck horde of crazed little people. It was not an altogether encouraging view, but Ed was still smiling gamely.

"Well, fellows," he said to the hubbub at large, "where are we going now? Who's got the car?"

I screamed into his ear, "Ed . . . Ed, maybe we better try to find our own transportation."

"Yeah . . . I said *yeah*. But, uh, where do we go?"

There seemed no answer to that, but suddenly one materialized. Rubbing the trophy might have produced him, who knows? But there suddenly was old Hussarian, right at Ed's elbow, looking pleased as Punch, wise and capable. We were moving again, in a southerly flow of bodies. Flash bulbs were popping, and small disembodied hands, thick as mosquitoes, hovered and settled over Ed.

"Get us out of here," he told Hussarian. "Where is Mike?"

"He eees with Bootler. You, Et Carney and Meek Kitz, *very great champions*."

"Fine, fine, Hussarian," said Ed, smiling at him. "Thank you very much."

"We go now," Hussarian said and began, with some incredible *suk* sense, to run through the crowd. Ed followed in his wash, hunkered over his trophies as if in a sleet storm, his blue-and-white Hawaiian shirt winking. I seriously followed Ed.

A block or two down the sidewalk, Hussarian cut left through three layers of bodies to the door of a cab he could not possibly have known was there. It was a small cab, but when we finally got the doors closed there were two enormous trophies and eight people in it: from where I sat in the back seat, my lap full of the new Mr. Universe and odds and ends of other people, I counted them. But at least we were behind metal and glass, and the Amateur Bodybuilding Champion of the World was no longer in any danger of being trampled to death.

As the driver shot through waves of people on the street, beginning an insane, rocketing, horn-blowing fling to the hotel, I managed to find Ed's hand and shake it. He was being kissed all over by every Arab in the car who could reach him with a mouth, and handled by the ones who couldn't.

"You done it."

Beleaguered as he was, he looked gone off, inside himself. "Yeah. You know, it's like a dream? The whole damn thing is like a dream," he said.

A dream was just what the whole thing must have felt mighty like to Mike Katz too—a bad one; dismally like the one he'd had the night before, but thickened with all the bitching minutiae of reality: the lower dais on the winner's platform—his, and Suemitsue's, the Japanese who took third place, a good two feet below Corney's; the moist looks of all those Iraqis who had expected him to win; the sinking feeling of *déjà vu* from having blown his year two years now in a row; and, mostly, the nasty little burr of having lost to an older, smaller man. And riding in

Prejudging, Medium Class, Baghdad

his own cab, less noisy and festive than Ed's, back to the Hotel Baghdad, Mike might well have been sick to death of dreams. He might have thought of his nice house on a wooded corner lot in suburban Hartford, of his antique car and his wife and son, and wished to be back there right *then*—out of this gone sour fantasy of minarets and mobs and weird water and unintelligible adulation. He might have felt all that, but if he did he didn't show it. Nor did he show any bitterness—not then, nor at the Cinema, nor later back at the hotel. Katz has a built-in sense of fairness, maybe from all the years he has spent at competitive sports, and he knew this would probably be the last crack Ed would have at the Universe. More important, he knew too that on this particular crack Ed had just flat deserved to win it.

He himself had looked good, he was sure of that—better than he had ever looked before: massive and defined, his waist down and his calves up from a year ago. And he had posed well, drawing his shots out longer, making transitions with more grace and picking his poses better than ever. It was just that Corney had looked better, and Mike knew it. Every muscle in Ed's forty-year-old body was out along its rim, close to its ultimate potential. Ed had finish: every part of him looked achieved and finished as a goddam apple. And his posing—well, there just wasn't anybody over here, or practically anywhere else, for that matter, who was going to beat Ed Corney's posing today.

Mike didn't begrudge Ed the title, and he didn't blame the water. So when he got back to the hotel, and the manager and the manager's family came running out to congratulate him for winning, if Mike was wishing like hell for the reality of that wooded lot and his twenty-one-inch color TV, he didn't let them know about it. And five or ten minutes later when our absurd clown car screeched up and Ed got out, shedding Arabs, to shake his hand, there was no kink in Mike's grin and nothing phony in his voice when he congratulated him. Mike might not have felt all that good, but he knew as well as anybody that losing and winning have nothing to do with dreams.

Ed Corney, on the other hand, was very, very happy—happy the way a man is who has just relieved himself of a year's worth of work. He felt successfully delivered, evacuated, and good. He ate loosely that night—garbaging up, as bodybuilders call it (though not as loosely as some do after a contest; nothing like, say, the way Ken Waller garbaged up about a year later in New York after he won the Mr. World, when he put down, in order, steak, veal and chicken dinners with three bottles of wine, and then went to a different restaurant and ate fourteen pancakes). And after he ate, he and Mike went out to the nightclub down the road that had for entertainment an international troupe of strippers billing themselves as ballet. The contest *had* in fact been televised all over the Middle East. People in Baghdad

The Crab

watched it at home and in bars and restaurants the way we watch the seventh game of the World Series, and Ed and Mike were celebrities in the nightclub. Halfway through her act, one of the strippers, a knockout French redhead, bellied over to Ed's table, and the two of them decided in different languages that they liked each other's moves. She went back to the hotel with him that night, and the next noon when the bus left for the airport she tried to get on it with him, having decided that Fremont, California, was as good a place as any to do ballet.

Things were definitely breaking for Ed: magically almost, over here in this place where magic still felt like a hell of a lot more than just entertainment for children. Certainly the way he and Mike had been fawned over and partied, the way they'd been appreciated, by everybody from the President to the shoe-shine boys outside the hotel—wasn't there some magic in that for a bouncer from Fremont, all of whose titles wouldn't even cash him a check back in the U.S.A., and who had been skinny more than once on luck and money? And beating out the big man, when nobody thought he could do it, and doing it this year when he had to? And even the girl in the nightclub, just when he was emptied out and loose and ready for that? And most of all, hadn't there been more than a little magic in him that afternoon at the Cinema? Hadn't he posed as if he owned the stage, as if no other bodybuilder had set foot on it before, moving as purely and naturally as water flowing, his fingers spreading to lead each new line, finding the lock just right on every shot? Lord, hadn't there ever been a little magic there.

Ed was happy all right that last night in Baghdad, and he planned to stay that way for a while. Things were breaking good. And just as Mike Katz knew about winning and losing, Ed Corney knew most of what there was to know about how fast they can break the other way.

Ten months after the contest in Baghdad, George and I were out in California, and one night we went up to see Corney at the nightclub where he works. He was standing outside the door, dressed in a pair of two-tone shoes, red knit pants, a tie and a red-and-white halter sweater. He looked very spiffy and polite and correct standing there, as though he had just taken a new girl to dinner and was waiting outside for her to come out of the ladies' room. He was holding a weighted police flashlight that he used for checking IDs and also for decking people whenever he had to do that. Mostly his job there, he said, was to turn away people under twenty-one and anyone in Levi's, and anyone who looked as if he might cause trouble in the club. He thought of himself as a sort of public-relations man, he said, and he always tried to avoid putting the thumb on people. But occasionally he had to, like that past Thursday when he had told a mean-drunk

Mr. Universe, 1972

"I won't do anything else until I win Mr. Universe. If I have to train ten years, I'm going to win it. I don't know why I say that because the education is just as important, but I could not he happy right now going out as a loser. I placed third in Mr. Universe last year. If I went out as a loser it would make the ten years I've spent in bodybuilding a complete waste."
—Mike Katz

Persian that he couldn't come in and the Persian hit him in the mouth. They had had to carry the guy away in an ambulance, and Ed felt bad about that, but it was part of the job, when push came to shove, to hit the other guy harder than he hit you.

Ed was very cheerful and glad to see us out there in front of the club, and after a while he took us inside and introduced us to some of his friends. The club was a candlelit, semi-badass place with Formica tables and a loud rock group. Most of the people in it knew Ed, and all of them were very polite around him. He bought us a drink and himself a Coke, and we stood up in front near the door and talked. He had gotten married, he said, after he got back from Iraq. His wife had gotten pregnant right away, but she had miscarried and they had split up after that. And he had just gotten out of the hospital two weeks ago. He had had a big operation on his knee, and the thing had cut him to 150 pounds, but he was back up to 170 now and training hard. He was coming to New York in two weeks for the Mr. World contest, he said, and he figured he'd be in top shape by then.

But mostly we talked about Baghdad, reminding each other of how much fun it had been and of all the crazy things that had happened. George had brought some pictures along, and Ed looked through them, looking at each one for a long time. His favorite was a picture taken at the Hotel Baghdad right after everybody had come back there from the contest. The hotel manager asked George to take it and it shows the manager and all his family standing with Ed and Mike in the corridor outside their room. Everybody is smiling. Everybody looks happy, but Ed looks the happiest of all.

We stayed at the club for a couple of hours, talking to Corney about Baghdad and watching him do his work. Then around two we had to leave to get a borrowed car back to San Francisco. We told Ed goodbye and said we'd see him in New York. When we drove out of the dark parking lot we could see Ed Corney Mr. Universe, back outside again, standing politely and alone in front of the door to the club, waiting for IDs to check.

Ed Corney outside Mr. Magooz, San Jose, Calif.

Eleven

Posing is the heart of the thing. Depending on how it is done, you can see in it either everything that is moving and beautiful and dignified about the display of a developed male body or everything that is ridiculous and embarrassing about it.

On its lowest level, posing is simply a technical matter of presenting the muscles, of emphasizing strong points and obscuring weak ones; and just beyond that it is an athletic skill like diving or hitting a baseball that requires timing and coordination. The great majority of bodybuilders never get beyond the point of athletic competence in their posing. Many do not even get there, and they, no matter how well developed, are always embarrassing to watch. The ones who are only competent can be interesting for one reason or another to see work, but one time is usually enough and you are hardly ever moved by them. But on its highest, most expressive level, as it is done by only a handful of people, physique posing is a kinetic form of art—requiring talent, imaginative and personal, turning on intuition—and no matter how many times you watch it performed there is always something new you can learn and feel from it.

Good posing, even great posing, is only so much movement, however interesting, unless it is displaying a first-rate physique. The physique gives the posing meaning, the posing gives expression to the physique, and the two have got to be equally finished and appropriate to each other for a routine to really grab and shake you the way the best ones can. When they are, there is nothing even remotely embarrassing or ridiculous in what you see.

What you see would look something like this: A man in a

Lou Ferrigno, growing up

pair of trunks (you would be unusual if at the end of the routine you could remember what color they were) gets up on a posing dais under a spotlight, and for a minute or two he flexes and shifts his body into different positions. The positions are called poses or shots. A normal show routine would include around fifteen of them, though some bodybuilders who work very fast, like Franco Columbu, might get thirty into the same length of time. In the best routines there are no major body weaknesses to cover up, so the poses would be about equally divided among front, side and back shots. Some of these would be standards, and a few, like the back double-biceps and the hulking front pose called "most muscular" or "the crab," are almost obligatory. Others would be personal variations of standard poses, and if it were one of the very best routines you would also see one or two poses that belong to that bodybuilder alone—that, because he fills them in a way no one else can fill them or has filled them, are his, no matter how many other people do them. The kneeling three-quarter back pose belongs to Arnold Schwarzenegger in this way. Larry Scott, one of the greatest posers ever, owned the front single-biceps pose before he retired, and now, six or seven years later, he still owns it.

The poses you'd see, since they have no cheating in them and do not strain for emotion, would be dramatic without being melodramatic, their drama coming naturally from the imaginative sureness of their composition. Each one would both surprise and gratify you—would seem an inevitable yet altogether new disposition of the body. Each would have its own emotional weight and character and yet be integrally bound to all the others in the routine. And finally, each pose, as well as the whole rou-tine, would seem transparent to you after it was over—as clear and simple as water.

Just as important as the poses themselves is the movement connecting them: all the best posing is an equal mixture of drama and grace, and it is the transitions that supply most of the grace. The movement in this routine would be unhurried, virile, smooth, carrying the body off the line of one pose just before the muscles begin to quiver from the strain of holding it, naturally and forcefully to the next. You would see no hesitation or thought; no stumbling or readjustment or compensation. All you would see is clear, lovely shifts, plunges and sweeps, some of them protracted and long-lined, others as choppy and brief as body punches, setting up the poses and carrying out of them again in what would seem to you the only possible way there is to do it.

A sense of things being done in the only way they can be done is one of the things you would feel, watching the routine; another is the clarity and impersonality of it. During very good posing you don't notice a bodybuilder's face any more than you do the color of his trunks. Neither do you, unless you are very new to watching, wonder what kind of man he is, or what he does for a living, or what his problems might be. In the AAU, the judges interview each of the Mr. America contestants before the competition, and the title is awarded partially on the basis of what they decide about—his character, or charm, some Atlantic City qualification that has nothing to do with what he is there for. The practice demeans bodybuilding competition and violates one of the things that is most unique and real about it: the fact that when both physique and posing are good enough they force the spectator to concentrate on a clean, impersonal, exciting geometry of circles and curves and on the movement tying it together, and to forget completely that it is a greased, nearly naked man, with charm or without, who is showing it to you.

The best posing is also completely without affectation or mannerisms. The way it was done by Grimek and Ross and Pearl and Scott, and the way it is done now by Arnold Schwarzenegger, Franco Columbu, Ed Corney and a few others, it seems, like all good art, artless. It isn't, of course; it is very highly contrived, but contrived in a way that blends grace and drama without any obtrusive magnification of either. That is the old way, the classic way, and in Corney and Schwarzenegger it may have reached its apogee.

There are two popular alternatives to that way now; both are flashier and easier to do, and both attract more and more young bodybuilders every year. One is a soft, choreographed kind of posing, much admired by women spectators. It is generally very graceful and melodramatic and is often performed to music. For its effects it relies on slow, mannered movements and moody, sinuous shots, many of them unflexed. Frank Zane is the leading proponent of this style. Zane is a nice man and an excellent body-builder with a small, beautifully proportioned physique that is as appropriate as any could be to this kind of posing. In his exhibitions he performs to music from *The Ten Commandments* and *2001*; and if, in watching, you get a slight sense of overripeness, of an overemphasis on grace, you at least know you are seeing this style of posing done as well as anybody does it.

The polar opposite of Zane's style is the one that, of present bodybuilders, Lou Ferrigno best represents. Ferrigno is six feet six and weighs around 275 pounds. Everything about him is enormous in the way boxcar couplings are enormous, and, of its kind, he has one of the best unfinished physiques in the history of bodybuilding. His posing (which is widely admired and copied in the East) is awesome and joyless, and lopsidedly dependent on his size. For his routine, Lou comes on stage looking angry and sleepy, as though the audience were a midnight burglar he'd surprised, and proceeds to crush out one massive shot after an-other. There

Lou Ferrigno, grown

is a sort of surly drama to what he does up there, but no more subtlety or grace than there is in the movement of road-building equipment.

Ferrigno is still in his early twenties, which is very young for a world-class bodybuilder. His potential is great, and it could be that his posing will take on art as his physique takes on finish, and that he will desert all the hulking, grimacing imitators he has now. It could also be that it won't. You can learn good posing only up to a certain point. Beyond that it is purely a matter of talent, and of intuition.

Arnold Schwarzenegger finished his routine, and the Olympia prejudging, with a crab shot that sent Raol into a frenzy of language behind us. Arnold grinned at the judges—it was the first time he had looked directly at them since he began—and left the stage without looking back, wiping down his shoulders and chest the way you do the flank of a lathered horse. Virginia and I sat for a couple of minutes without talking, she chewing on her lower lip and watching the ring of dampness that Arnold had left behind on the stage.

We had just seen a posing routine. In fact, we had just seen three—his, Franco's and Serge Nubret's—any one of which could serve, on film, say, as a wordless definition of what bodybuilding is all about.

Virginia shifted and laid her head back on the seat. It was the first move I'd seen her make in fifteen minutes.

"Why aren't they famous? Why doesn't everybody know about this?"

"They just haven't gotten around to it. And bodybuilding has given itself a rotten press. You ready to go? It's five-thirty."

"I feel like I was just hit in the eyes with a goddam ax."

"He'd like to hear that. Why don't we go backstage and you can tell him that."

"No. I don't want to meet him—just dream about him. It's sad, Chawes—that more people don't know. When you see it like that there's nothing, you know, *dingy* about it, or id-ish, or vain, or any of those things I thought it would be."

"The best ones do that for you. When they pose they cut right through all the myths and the bad organization and the tacky magazines, all that chalky feet stuff, and show you what the thing is really like."

"Chalky feet stuff?"

"It's just something I remember from when I first started going to these things."

"Did you like them then?"

"Not at first. I didn't know how to look as well as you do. We'd better move it if you're going out."

A B A

"They must be awfully lonely. Doing that beautiful thing and nobody around to appreciate it."

"There are people around who do. There'll be a couple of thousand of them here tonight."

I stood up and handed Virginia her coat. She took it but didn't get up. She sat there with her lovely head on the back of the seat, looking up at me.

"Will he be that good tonight?"

"Maybe better. The Oak loves an audience."

"I've decided I'm going to come." She stood up then and put on her coat. '

"I thought you couldn't."

"I can."

We walked up the aisle toward the dark front of the Brooklyn Academy of Music. Down on the stage they were setting up for the show. The bodybuilders would have a couple of hours now to go out and get something careful to eat, though most of them probably wouldn't.

"Chawes?" said Virginia. "You know what I said about Elizabethan music? Well, that was dumb. It's not a bit like that. Not at all."

Frank Zane

Twelve
Mr. Olympia No. 4

Franco was nearly perfect. He was in the best shape of his life and he thought he could win, defeating the bar-fight maxim that a good big man will always beat a good small one. As it happened, he did beat one big man, and on another night he might have beaten the other one. But tonight Franco was followed not by another routine at all, but by an epiphany—a performance that revealed in the space of a couple of minutes, to everyone in the audience who was watching well enough, all there is to know about bodybuilding; allowed them to see it entire, like a pasture from a helicopter.

Like so much of what he does, in posing trunks and out of them, Arnold Schwarzenegger's routine that night turned on a single moment, a single brilliant intuition. He has a flair for them. Like earlier that day, for instance. At just about the same time Serge Nubret's limousine was pulling up in front of the Brooklyn Academy, the Oak turned off of Sixth Avenue onto Forty-fourth Street in mid-Manhattan and strolled down the block toward his hotel. The Algonquin Hotel to be exact—in whose small, exquisite lobby generations of literati have sat on the red sofas, ringing for tea or gin; in its dining room and lobby the Oak and the other bodybuilders staying there were pondered like literary symbols. It was a brilliant September morning, the rectangle of sky between the buildings on Forty-fourth Street was a hard enamel blue, and the air on the street crackled with light. The Oak turned the corner and walked down the block like a wave breaking. He was wearing emerald-green shorts. His centaur legs were a bright copper color from a new coat of Tan-

"I find out which poses they really like. That's why I don't have a specific posing routine, because you never know what they like and what they don't. Sometimes you think a routine is good but the applause is going down. Like Franco explained, he did one shot coming up for triceps from the side and the sound went down, so he cut the shot. You have to be very flexible in these things. You have to listen. When you hit the most-muscular and they start screaming, you know they like the more freaky poses, so you keep hitting it again and maybe hold it longer to get the cuts out more. You know then they like the drama shots and you can forget the symmetrical stuff."
—Arnold Schwarzenegger

"Not many bodybuilders dress up the way we do. The reason I dress up, it really makes me proud. And Natalie. I have my clothes tailored for myself, and I like to show. It's like you have a collection and it's part of you and you like to show people. It's my hard work—to keep my body in shape, and hers. And we like to dress up and we like to show. We go to a place and people talk and turn and they laugh about it and some of them make jokes about it, and all this makes us feel even more proud of it. There's no better thing than working with something that you really own. I can have a beautiful racing car and somebody can steal it, but your body—your body is the only thing you really own."
—Tony Roma

"Tony goes with me to ladies' stores because I like him to tell me what clothes I should put on, and they just laugh and laugh 'cuz they just can't stand the bodybuilders. And we in turn, we laugh at them because we know that that's so lousy. We just laugh at them . . . it's a ball. I have a ball every time we go out. Everyplace we go everybody stares at us like we're men from Mars or something like that. I think bodybuilding's a great thing. I'm really into it all the way, you know. I like watching men work out. And I help Tony all the time—I sit on his back for donkey calf-raises; I give him incentive."
—Natalie Raposa

Arnold in the Crab

Tony Roma & Natalie Raposa, the Algonquin Hotel

in-a-Minute. A car full of his buddies turned onto Forty-fourth and slowed beside him, and then suddenly the whole street was alive with bodybuilders, driving up in cars, coming out of the hotel. The doorman and taxi drivers gaped: these huge people seemed conjured from the sparkling air. There was laughter from the car and a shout as it pulled off. Out in the street behind it the Oak whooped mightily and kicked at the fender. There were maybe a dozen pairs of eyes in front of the Algonquin Hotel, and all of them watched his carved leg wink outward in a high floating punt that seemed to catch the fancy New York morning smack in the bustle. It was a perfectly intuited fusion of moment with motion, of a physical act with a collective state of mind—as spontaneous and unpredictable as bodybuilding itself—and it cracked the instant open like an egg on a pan. Possibility ran in the street. Blasé, the Oak went upstairs to change. There was nothing new to him about this sort of labor; a couple of years ago he made a movie here called *Hercules in New York*.

So later, backstage at the Academy, listening to the crowd and knowing he needed something, some little exactly right something to follow Franco with, Arnold Schwarzenegger simply reached down and came up with it.

What happens is this:

In a madness of noise, an ear-splitting, wall-shaking tumult of noise, he takes the stage, his face radiant, and shows the audience and judges—a single leg. It is the leg he injured a few months earlier when a posing platform in South Africa collapsed with him, and he wants them to see that it is as good as ever. He turns it languidly, showing the elegant complexity of his calf. Then he cuts to a front double-biceps—a pose that shows the entire front of the body. From zoom to pan, from detail to mind-blowing whole. It's as sharp and right as that kick outside the hotel, and it impales the crowd. A sort of moaning begins out

front as they take in the softball-sized biceps, the long, deep pectoral slabs, the yawning latissimus dorsi—all that carved, intricate bulk at once. He holds it, his body straight, his arms flexed at shoulder height, a pure, lovely, demanding pose that demonstrates both his size and symmetry at once.

From there he goes in a crunch of arms to the most muscular, turning his chest, arms and shoulders into an anatomy-chart splay of veins and cuts, and maddening the audience. Then to his own three-quarter back shot, a one-arm side back, a back double-biceps, a side back with the other arm—each movement long, pure, uncluttered. It is posing at its driest and shapeliest, mixing grace and drama without cheating or excess and with no taint of the effete or the grotesque. It makes you feel, in the dignity and beauty of its finish, that you have never watched posing before.

And as he lays these perfect poses on the crowd, the luck and strain and glamour and joy of doing it are right up there on Arnold's face. All over his features. No preoccupation here, Jack, no dark, motivated, Nubretish absence of expression here. He is as into this as the ravening crowd—glistening, flexing, swooping from shot into marvelous shot. These are his people, and this is his thing, at his moment. He is Nureyev in London, Caruso at La Scala, Babe Ruth at Wrigley Field pointing his bat—a king, with a court, at the top of his art.

When he finishes with another most muscular, throws up his hands and bounds off the dais out of the spotlight, the deafening mixture of screaming, moaning and applause that has not sagged, not once, since he came out takes on a strangely wrenched quality, almost of lament. Nearly to the stage exit, Arnold stops in the half-dark. He listens to the audience, his head cocked, smiling in the shadows. Then he looks back at the dais, hesitates, and returns.

"Number one, it runs through my mind it is very obvious I am the king. Then I thought to the audience, just keep screaming now because you're going to see the poses for just a few minutes here, so eat your hearts out."
—Arnold Schwarzenegger

Thirteen
The Terrain, 1980

In 1971 and before, the only connection you could find between competitive bodybuilding and the rest of America was the gym-rat. The gym-rat was maybe eighteen and you could locate him in the culture, if you looked hard enough, anywhere from the central middle class on down. He had puffy, undefined arms, bad legs, and he tended to burp a lot in public from all the Tiger's Milk he drank every night before bed. He was the one—the only one, really—who bought the vitamin supplements, the "crusher" grip-exercisers, the posters of Larry Scott and the chest programs of Dave Draper that were advertised then exclusively in the back pages of comic books and girly magazines. And he was the only one in America in 1972—the *only one*—who knew who Arnold Schwarzenegger was.

Muscles were cheap as dirt in 1972—in fact, except to the gym-rats, you couldn't give them away. Now they are big business, not just for a couple of men with the same last name as was the case in '72, but for what sometimes seems to be half the country. It's not that the goods are any different from what they were in '72—the goods are still books and mail-order programs, gym memberships, vitamin supplements and bodybuilding equipment—it's just that they are *everywhere* now, being bought and used not only by the gym-rat but by his parents, his grandparents, even his girlfriend.

For better or worse, in the past eight years competitive bodybuilding has been assimilated, adapted and merchandised for general consumption. Your average stockbroker still doesn't put on skimpy little trunks on Sunday and hop onto a posing dais in a public place, but the chances are very good now that he exercises with weights, and almost as good that he does those exercises the way he has heard or read that Arnold does them.

Valerie and Boyer Coe

Rachel McLish

The crowd, Miss Olympia, Philadelphia

Danny Padilla

Lou Ferrigno and *Stay Hungry* director
Bob Rafelson

Why? What happened here in eight years? Well Arnold himself happened, for one thing, glamourizing muscles for the first time since Sandow, and—by feeding and watering his own in places like Elaine's and Dan Tana's, in the company of people like Jackie Onassis, Andy Warhol, and Jamie Wyeth—making them chic. And big Louis Ferrigno happened as a kind of star in his own right, snarling and looming and throwing things around every week on television as the Hulk; as did Franco Columbu, through television's World's Strongest Man competition and a number of television commercials that brilliantly engaged his good looks, his cuddly Sardinian accent and his elfin personality. And of course fitness happened—in an authentic craze of Americans running down highways and beaches, over golf courses and parks, even in the City of New York; and very soon the craze, as is always the case in this country, became a "look." *The* look. No more bearded, cerebral and anguished. No more rich, thin and careless. No more bisexual, bicoastal and arty. All at once the look was fit—and what are muscles, after all, ran the thinking, but the ornaments of fitness, the hard-won jewelry of the good life? If you doubt this fashion exists, by the way, just go down to one of the big New York model agencies like Zoli or Elite and compare pictures of their top models in 1972, men and women, to their present stars. You will notice that all those pretty people seem to have swollen subtly over the years, to have put on an average of five to ten golden, muscular pounds. A lot of the men look like little pouting Arnolds, and there are many more Cheryl Tiegses and Christie Brinkleys pictured now than Twiggys.

Anyway, all of that happened and other things as well, and suddenly—at once, it seemed—bodybuilding had "arrived" in America, come up out of the basement and taken a seat in the living room. Now it is among us variously: still in its old pure forms of sport and art—and we will look later at how these have changed and at some of the people who have changed them—but more visibly in its diffused, newly adapted shapes of big business, fitness, fashion and entertainment.

If you had wanted to see all those new shapes together at one time in one place, all jostling and crowding each other, pushing the poor gym-rats back up against the sills, you could not have picked a better place than the Sheraton Hotel in Philadelphia over the last weekend of August, 1980. That was the site of the first annual International Bodybuilding Convention, as well as the first IFBB Miss Olympia competition.

The *Miss* Olympia competition, you wonder? Women? What do women have to do with bodybuilding? In 1972 the answer would have been nothing; arguably, that is still the answer. But there they were in Philadelphia that hot weekend, one of the more eye-catching of the new shapes.

The weekend was produced by an organization called The Association, also new. The Association is made up of Arnold Schwarzenegger, Franco Columbu, George Snyder and Bill Drake. It

Georgia Fudge

Kelly Everts, Brooklyn, 1973

Dumbell flyes

Patsy Chapman pumping up

Carla Dunlop, curls

Auby Paulick

is a cheerfully profit-making organization established to provide special services such as financing, promotion and discounts on supplements and equipment to gyms and health clubs across the country. There was no such organization in 1972 because gyms and health clubs then were not doing well enough nationally to afford or need one. Now they are. For example, in 1972 the Health and Tennis Corporation, owner of the largest chain of gyms in the country, had fewer than 50 locations nationally; now it has 180 locations, and its sales have gone up 30 percent a year since 1972.

The combination Convention/Miss Olympia contest in Philadelphia was the first event produced by the Association, and it was produced with finesse and style. In 1972 everything would have gone wrong, but it wouldn't have mattered: the gym-rats, who would have been the only people there anyway, wouldn't have cared if anything *happened*, much less happened right, as long as they were able to stare unbothered at the stars and occasionally take a picture of one. But this was 1980, and an event produced for and by the new big-business shape of bodybuilding, and it was *crisp*. The format was this: On Saturday morning after registration there were two seminars given by Arnold and Franco. Saturday afternoon, while the prejudging of the Miss Olympia contestants went on, there were more seminars, by Frank Zane, the reigning Mr. Olympia, John Balik, and Franco's wife, Anita Columbu. That night there was a banquet, followed by the Miss Olympia show and later by dancing to a loud rock band. And on Sunday there were three more seminars, given by Boyer Coe and Steve Michalik, Robbie Robinson and Mike Katz, and Mike Mentzer and Danny Padilla. Nearly 2,000 people, not half of them gym-rats, paid seventy-five dollars a head to attend all this. It was an interesting crowd that filled the Sheraton Hotel that weekend, much better heeled and better educated than it would have been eight years before. Though network television, male bodybuilding's best friend since '74, had elected to wait and see about this female thing, local TV was there in force, as well as a number of national print journalists. Ben Weider, head of the International Federation of Bodybuilders, the sanctioning organization for the competition, was there. So was his brother Joe. There was some glamour, a few voyeurs, a few researchers and writers—and a slew of flourishing bodybuilding businessmen, who spent most of their time in the basement.

In the basement of the Philadelphia Sheraton you could locate and observe the true foundation of all the newly well-organized and well-staged activity going on above it: the rampant merchandising of muscles. Down there, in an area about the size of half a football field, were the "Exhibits"—booths set up by makers of equipment, purveyors of supplements and vitamins, gym owners, and the star bodybuilders themselves from upstairs, appearing down here at their booths from time to time as writers of books and pamphlets and salesmen of personalized T-shirts—everybody happily turning the new body dollar together, in an atmosphere something like a Baghdad *suk*.

Check-pose

Ben Weider and friends

Stacey Bentley before prejudging

Franco and Anita had a booth from which they were selling T-shirts and the products of their prodigious literary output: five booklets and seven books. Frank Zane, his mother at his side, was selling his very good book, *The Zane Way to a Beautiful Body*, booklets, and prints and posters of himself. Boyer Coe was selling his book and booklets. And so on. In 1972 there were, so far as I know, no books on bodybuilding available nationally. Now, according to Joe Weider, who should know, there are more than sixty. Joe Weider is a nice, droll man with watery blue eyes who has done much for bodybuilding and vice versa. His California corporation, which sells supplements and equipment, was one of the few successful ones of its kind in 1972. Though there are many more now, Joe's own volume of business has increased by 600 percent since then. His magazine *Musclebuilder/Power* had a circulation of 80,000 in '72; now it has over 350,000. Like a few other people down there in the basement, Joe Weider had been around bodybuilding for a long time—since it was small and furtive, living full time in the basement and darting around the back pages of magazines to make a buck. And seeing it now in all its new confident shapes, striding around with big clean grins, firm handshakes and money in the bank, gave Joe and his brother Ben and the rest of those few a kind of pleasure and pride that the others in the basement, the Johnny-Come-Latelys, couldn't begin to feel.

Not that the others were hurting. Most of them were exercise equipment manufacturers—like Corbin-Gentry, maker of nine hulking "biomechanically synchronized machines," a number of which were on exhibit—and practically no exercise equipment manufacturer, or seller, in America today is hurting. Take Corbin-Gentry, for example. In the three years its line has existed, sales of the machines doubled in the second year and tripled in the third. Or take Nautilus, the world's largest exercise machine manufacturer: Its business has doubled annually since 1972 and Nautilus facilities around the country are now multiplying at the rate of twelve to fifteen new installations per *week*. Or take Sears, Roebuck, whose sales of exercise equipment is up over 300 percent since 1972; or York Barbell Company, the country's largest manufacturer of free iron weights, whose sales are up 250 percent since then.

There were so many machines showing themselves off in the basement that the place looked like a problem in solid geometry. There were machines from World Class Gym Equipment, and machines from Cam II that use pressurized air for resistance. From Iron Company there was a computer you put your finger in and it told you how fit you were. And there were the flashiest machines of all, the Dyna-Cam Line from Dynamics Health Equipment, a sponsor of the show in Philadelphia: fancy orange Naugahyde and gleaming chrome machines into one of which Franco Columbu put his entire self on Friday night and proceeded to get lost.

Everybody had a fine time in the basement of the Sheraton, playing with the machines, talking to the author-bodybuilders, and smelling the new, heady aroma of arrival everywhere. But to the

215

old-timers at least, the best thing about the basement was that they could leave it—walk out of it at the end of Saturday afternoon on their way, By God, upstairs to the ballroom.

Earlier in the day Arnold's and Franco's seminars had been well attended, each of them drawing over a thousand people. That's a *thousand* people—to hear Arnold on The Psychology of Bodybuilding, and Franco on Strength and Injuries. Like bodybuilding itself, Arnold exists in a lot of forms nowadays—roles that he shifts in and out of as easily as he does his custom-made Morty Sills jackets. As he was to prove only a month later, he is still one of the world's finest competitors. He is also, at different times, a movie and television actor, a successful author, a tough, shrewd business entrepreneur, a loyal friend to dozens of people, and the magnetic, if sometimes arrogant and idiosyncratic, chief spokesman for bodybuilding. He is, too, a polished and convincing speaker, particularly on the subject of winning. Winning is Arnold's life song, his key to the secret door, and his talk on it that morning, on setting goals and never having doubts and stripping away negative influences, was more than just good motivational rhetoric—it was a window into the complex machinery that has made him one of the most effective people alive.

Franco's talk was polished too, if a little eccentric. He dominates the stage as fully as Arnold does, with his unfaked cuteness, his manliness and good spirits. Watching and listening to him, you find yourself smiling along with whatever private joke it is that keeps Franco's touch on life so amused and exuberant. Whatever else may have changed, these two men—the cream of their crop—have not; they've only grown into themselves. And they don't even seem to have aged since 1972.

Just after noon the prejudging for the Miss Olympia contest began. There were twenty-one girls entered, all but five of whom had won titles previously during the short two- or three-year period in which there have been titles to win in female bodybuilding. This was by far the most prestigious competition to date and the richest, with $10,000 in total prize money and a trip to Venezuela for the first five finishers. I had not seen a women's contest before, and I wanted to keep an open mind. If the idea of it seemed a little *wrong* to me somehow, like the idea of a tits and ass competition for men, say— well, I was ready to be shown otherwise.

Trying to get a slant on how the competitors felt about what they did, I talked to a few girls before the prejudging: to a gorgeous Dane named Anniqua Fors who didn't feel much about it at all beyond liking it; to the current Miss Long Island, Kyle Newman, who got into it, she said, because she likes competition and because she heard there was money in it; and to Patsy Chapman, a pretty black girl who started lifting weights in high school, and carried it on into college at Michigan State where she was then a senior, sort of because it made her feel good and helped her with other sports.

So there *weren't* any burning Arnoldian phrases about the body as art form, or any soft, moving, Corney-like monologues on making one thing perfect in an imperfect world—so what, I told myself; it's all new, and the girls are nervous: wait for the prejudging. Just before the prejudging the girls pumped up in a little room barely large enough to hold them all. They came in one by one, dressed in caftans and warmup suits, looking shyly at each other, Making up

217

Patsy Chapman

Suzy Green

Rachel McLish, Suzy Green, and Georgia Fudge at prejudging

Prejudging

most of them, and smiling. Most of them were in their early and middle twenties, but there were a couple of older ones: a tall, handsome thirty-four-year-old gym owner from Florida named Geor-gia Fudge, and ageless Kellie Everts from Brooklyn of the eye-boggling bustline, the lascivious smile and the scarlet dagger fingernails, who was strutting her stuff on the stage of the Brooklyn Academy of Music back in 1973 between weight classes at the first *Mr.* Olympia contest I ever attended. Kellie and Georgia did not look shyly at anyone.

Patsy Chapman came in and started doing serene toe raises against the wall. The Danish girl was deadlifting, dressed in a caftan. A lovely oral surgeon's assistant named Corrine Machado in a fuschia bikini was being oiled up by her boyfriend. More girls arrived, among them an infectiously cheerful, nut-brown little blonde named Auby Paulick from Birmingham, Michigan. Auhy Paulick looks like her name ought to be Tammie, like she says "shucks" a lot, enjoys practical jokes, and wakes up singing "Oh What a Beautiful Morning." She is your sturdy farm wife carried to an honestly awesome extreme of strong curves and spooned into a white bikini. Auby hogged the mirror for a while, flexing her flamboyant little legs and chuckling, then she bounced over to the big blue Corbin-Gentry lat machine and commenced posing for eager old Russ Warner, the bodybuilding photographer. And just then the favorite walked in—Rachel McLish, the U.S. Women's Bodybuilding champ from Harlingen, Texas. Rachel had on a halter top and a blue skirt; she has Iong curly hair, huge Byzantine eyes, and a lithe, well-defined body. It is a body with finish, a body sort of like Frank Zane's, where the parts enjoy an elegant relationship to the whole, and along with Auby Paulick's, it seemed to me to be the class body in the room. But was it sexy, you want to know—Rachel McLish's body, or Auby Paulick's? Or how about the Dane's? How *sexy* were they? Well, not very—not to me at least and I'm not particularly hard to please—and that was what kept bothering me as I watched all those girls pumping and oiling up and check-posing in the mirror. Most of them had nice bodies; a few had beautiful bodies, none more muscular really than a world-class female sprinter's or swimmer's. But not one of those bodies made me want to sell my house and barn to touch it, and that plain puzzled me. You're carping, I told myself—it's probably the context. Besides, who said it *has* to be sexy? Wait, I told myself again, for the prejudging.

The prejudging was held finally in a long, thin conference room full of official observers, press, and judges. Male prejudgings have a smell to them—a strong acrid smell made up of nervousness, pride, sweat, and baby oil. Almost as soon as the women filed in and took their places in front of the long table of four men and three women judges you could notice that the smell was interestingly different—still acrid but sweeter and more tentative, as if it had in it some of the touching tractability and eagerness to please that soon became apparent in the contestants. There were three rounds in the judging,

Rachel McLish, Cammy Lusko, and Auby Paulick

Deborah Diana

Georgia Fudge

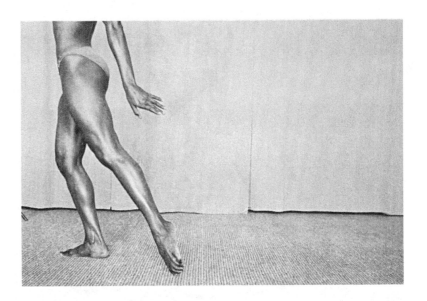

followed by a pose-off between six finalists for the top five places. In the first round each woman was observed relaxed from the front and rear and each side; in the second she demonstrated six compulsory poses; and in the third she had one minute to perform her own free routine of poses. It was this third round that was duplicated for the presentation or performance of the contest that night.

So . . . they stood there as a group at first, relaxed, some with their arms held out wide to the sides as the men do, accommodating imaginary lats, and all of them smiling at Christine Zane, Frank's wife and the head judge. Patsy Chapman looked calm and dignified. Auby Paulick looked juiced and trembly. Rachel McLish looked the best in repose, more streamlined and polished than the others, her pretty face set in a Miss America look of ingratiating, thoughtless delight.

With the posing lights on them you could see washboard ridges along some of their abdomens, ridges that would have driven Rubens crazy. You could notice that most of them had unusually small, and in some cases no, breasts; and that in every case their legs were their best feature, the muscles there looking athletic and natural. (*Some* of the legs, it should be said, were works of art—Lynn Conkwright's, Stacey Bentley's, Auby's, Rachel's.) Later, during the compulsory and free posing rounds, you could notice other things: that the best of their biceps and narrow lats were not as well developed as a normally athletic boy's, that there was practically no development at all in any of their backs or triceps or forearms, that deltoid "caps" throw off the natural symmetry of a woman's body—things like that. But I didn't need the posing to make up my mind about this particular new shape of modern bodybuilding. Watching those women all in a line when they first came out and stood there in the lights, shifting their feet, flexing as much as they could get away with and smiling nervously at Christine Zane, even before Christine told the first one to "make a quarter turn to the right, please," beginning the long, long afternoon of judging, I suddenly realized that I found all of this seriously depressing.

Legs, Patsy Chapman

You might not. But underneath whatever else you might feel watching women labor under a want of testosterone to show you the stringy muscles they have developed despite that want, you will likely have to feel a little sorry for them.

Frank Zane put the whole thing into an obscure nutshell that night at the show. There were fifteen hundred people at the show and the banquet that preceded it—all of them dressed to the nines and ready to be entertained. They were not all female bodybuilding fans—a lot of them were there to see the top male bodybuilders with whom Arnold and the rest of the Association had wisely decided to leaven the evening. But no matter what they were there for, they got their money's worth. In terms of production, the Miss Olympia show was light-years beyond what was being done in 1972. It *moved*, for one thing. It was intelligently arranged, well choreographed, lit and scored. In short, it was fun to watch, and that could rarely if ever have been said eight years ago about any bodybuilding show. It was also, this show, something more than well mounted: it was for me, and I think a lot of people there, an affecting and fascinating mixture of bodybuilding's old and new shapes.

Appropriately enough, it began with a few old timers—guys over forty—posing, and then popped to Ron Teufel, a blocky, crowd-pleasing young comer with a flashy routine. I had never seen Teufel before and I asked Frank Zane what he thought of him. Frank was sitting next to me at one of the banquet tables with his mother on his other side.

"Okay," said Frank. "Except for his back and his rear delts . . . Otherwise he's good."

Steve Michalik posed after Teufel. Michalik was the AAU Mr. America in 1972. I got to know him in '73, liked him, and quoted him at length in the old text of this book. Since then Steve has had some bad luck; he was hoping this year to start a comeback. "Looks a little heavy," said Frank Zane, and Michalik did, though his posing is still classical and lovely to watch.

Buster Crabbe, the old movie Flash Gordon, was introduced next. Crabbe at that time represented Dynamics Health Equipment Company, maker of the Dyna-Cam machines and a sponsor of the show. Talk about fascinating yokings of the old with the new: here came this leathery, wizened old ex-Flash Gordon out of the audience to stand at the podium preceding a female bodybuilding show, to thank Joe Weider and Dyna-Cam for his being there that night, and then to tell a long, old-fashioned Carole Lombard story that fizzled—in that ambitious young audience—and went out. Just as fascinating—the strangeness beginning to pile up now—was the act that followed Crabbe. In a display of the new bodybuilding entertainment, Boyer Coe and his wife, Valerie, a bodybuilder also, performed a dual posing exhibition, a sort of dance with poses thrown in, during which Boyer picked his wife up a lot and tossed her around. The audience loved it, and Bill Dobbins, a good young bodybuilding

Ron Mangum and Craig Cole

Suzy Green

Patsy Chapman

The new Mr. Olympia, Franco Columbu

Couples

writer who works for Joe Welder's magazines, called it later in print "the high point of the exhibitions." Well . . . Valerie Coe is a pretty, graceful woman and Boyer one of the best bodybuilders alive, but their performance, with its emotional awkwardness and nightclub triteness of movement, seemed to me to obscure both of them.

Ben Welder, president of the IFBB, came out after the Coes, congratulated himself and his organization variously, and officially opened the first Miss Olympia contest. There were more male posing routines thrown in at various points during the female competition. Some were old routines, and some were new—like Danny Padilla's, done with humor and zest by the sawed-off, massive Padilla to the song *Short People.* Even the old routines had some new elements to them. Frank Zane, who, as the current Mr. Olympia, posed last—following Padilla, Mike Katz, Robbie Robinson, Mike Mentzer and Boyer Coe—poses with more strength and tension than he did in 1972, and now to deafening music. And Mike Katz—the not-quite Mr. Universe of the original *Pumping Iron* who was there that weekend both as a judge and to begin, like Steve Michalik, a comeback—did his routine with newly curled hair, a new Rodin *Thinker* pose and less muscle than in '73; but his big chest, his endearing presence on stage and his dignity were the same. The women, in the meantime, were more fun to watch than they had been at the prejudging but, with one exception, not much. Rachel McLish, who had already won the contest, seemed confused and mannered in front of the big crowd, and Patsy Chapman seized up and groped. Stacey Bentley, Corrine Machado and Lynn Conkwright, who placed fifth, fourth and third respectively, were much better than in the afternoon, and so was Georgia Fudge, the thirty-four-year-old Floridian, who posed that night with nice understated drama. But the star of the night show was Auby Paulick, who took second place in the competition. Grinning and singing along with her music, doing handstands and cartwheels and finishing with a leg split, looking out frowsy and starry-eyed and pleased as punch at the howling audience, Auby was something spectacular—a sort of gymnast-dancer-showwoman with great legs, a ton of personality and a hard stomach, and something I would pay to go back to see. But her muscles had nothing to do with it.

Women's bodybuilding has arrived. Along with dual posing and effective staging, along with bodybuilding businessmen and the explosion of machines and health-food products and muscle literature, along with the few male bodybuilders who are now stars and the many who now make good money through TV commercials and movie spots and endorsements of the muscle products that are selling like hotcakes to an entire country bent on looking better—along with all that, women's bodybuilding is part of the new terrain. It may, as some people are saying, come to be the dominant feature of that terrain; that will depend on how well it can be marketed to the general public—on how many women can be made to want to look like Auby Paulick or Rachel McLish, and, to a lesser degree, on how

Terri LeCicero, Doug Weintz, and Cynthia Sabia

Mike Mentzer

many men can be made to want to sleep with them.

That marketing might be accomplished immediately—a lot of smart people are betting it will be. It could, like the selling of male bodybuilding, take a long time. And it might never happen. What if you watched a quarterback throw a pass over and over to an open receiver—nothing else, just throw a completed pass over and over to a receiver standing alone downfield? Bodybuilding, male or female, is by its nature almost as static and repetitive as that. It is standardized personal performance, a little like bullfighting without the bull, and what makes the great, even some simply good, male bodybuilders able to transfix and move you is not how they deviate from the standard (for the best bodybuilders have all been classical posers with classical bodies), or how they juice up their acts, but how directly and cleanly they connect, as they pose, with the subconscious symbolism of muscles—the age-old, mythic underpinnings of male strength. It is that connection, when it is made, that raises male bodybuilding above bizarre visual entertainment or the sexual strutting of plumage and, occasionally, carries it into art. It may not matter much in the new terrain, but all the marketing in the world can't provide that connection for the women.

That was what Frank Zane put into an unusual nutshell for me. As well as anyone there that weekend, Frank understands what is going on in bodybuilding in 1980. He was around before Arnold Schwarzenegger arrived in this country, and he has won the Mr. Olympia title three times since Arnold retired. Early in the evening show, as we watched Anniqua Fors, the beautiful Danish girl, pose, he leaned over to me and said, "You familiar with Carl Jung?"

"Yeah."

"Well I don't think there's an archetype for this," Frank said.

Frank Zane

Mike Katz

Fourteen
The Sport and the Art, 1980

When George Butler and I set out in the summer and fall of 1980 to determine what had happened in bodybuilding since we first looked into it, we thought we had two separate jobs: to identify and characterize the new forces and people in the sport by getting onto the contest circuit again, and to track down the people and forces depicted in the original *Pumping Iron* and find out what had happened to them. To our surprise, the jobs turned out to be the same. In order to get acquainted with the new competitors, to see how competition and organizational structure had changed, and to learn exactly what changes had been wrought in the sport and the art, George and I went to two competitions together and one each separately; we also went to gyms, old and new, and to equipment and nutritional-product manufacturers. And everywhere we went, though we found the landscape distinctly altered and more populated, we kept finding the same people and forces controlling it that we had found in 1972. Over the past eight years, we learned, bodybuilding had grown like a glacier—broadening at the base while remaining essentially unchanged at the top. Everything and nothing was different. Joe and Ben Weider still called the shots in marketing and competitive organization respectively; Ed Corney was still the best poser, and Arnold Schwarzenegger the best bodybuilder alive.

Arnold proved he was that this year by emerging from a five-year retirement and winning a controversial Mr. Olympia title in Sydney, Australia—his seventh. By way of further making the point that nothing has really changed. Franco Columbu will probably try for the title next year, and he will very likely take it, as he did in 1976 following Arnold's retirement. As with Arnold, and bodybuilding in general, much is different with Franco since 1972—he is a chiropractor now with a successful practice; he is a veteran TV personality and

Two scenes from the movie *Pumping Iron:*

Arnold in ballet studio

Franco in Sardinia

star of a series of television commercials, and he is a millionaire—yet much remains the same: he is still the undisputed clown prince of bodybuilding, its freest and blithest spirit, its strongest practitioner, and the best small man in the business. Even Sergio Oliva, the great Cuban bodybuilder who won the Olympia title in 1967, '68, and '69, has recently lumbered back into competition, and is presently capable, I am told, of beating anyone.

Think about it and try to come up with another sport in which the same three men (four with Frank Zane, who was Mr. Universe in 1968 and Mr. Olympia in '77, '78, and '79) who were the best eleven years ago are still the best whenever they choose to compete.

But it isn't only as competitors that the same old people continue in evidence in bodybuilding. You see them now, as well, as teachers of expensive seminars, contest promoters and judges, and salesmen of their own products—wearing a variety of the new bodybuilding suits, and sometimes two or three at once. As I have mentioned, separately and together George Butler and I went to four contests this summer and fall. At one or more of them we saw practically every bodybuilder dealt with in the original edition of this book, with two notable exceptions: Serge Nubret, who has taken his muscles and gone home to France, and Lou Ferrigno, who has Hulked out of the sport and into serial TV. Of the four major characters in the original book, Arnold was at three of the contests, twice as a promoter and once as a competitor; Ed Corney was also at three, once to sell his goods and twice as a competitor; Franco was at two, giving a seminar and selling his products at one, and supporting Arnold and looking over the competition for next year at the other; and Mike Katz was at three—to produce, to judge and hold a seminar, and to compete.

It was wonderful having those old competitors and friends everywhere we went, performing a variety of roles. It provided us with familiar access to what was going on, as well as informed, often wry, and rarely objective evaluations of it. It brought our jobs together, and allowed us to see the old and the new side by side and through each other—good perspectives from which to report the state of a sport and art at once radically altered and unchanged after eight years.

The first contest we went to was the Best in New England Body Building Championships held in Connecticut at the Hamden High School Auditorium on a Saturday in the middle of August. It was produced by Mike Katz. In size and feel it was not unlike Ed Jubinville's annual Mr. East Coast contest in Holyoke, Massachusetts, which is described in the text of this book and was the first bodybuilding competition George and I went to together. Some of the competitors we met at that first contest were in Mike's, eight years later, and one of them won second place.

Ed Jubinville was also there, as head judge. This was an AAU contest. Back in 1972 the AAU was, along with the IFBB, NABBA, and the WBBG, one of four separate sanctioning organizations for bodybuilding competition, each of which worked against the others, creating for years a chaos of mutually exclusive procedures and similarly-named titles. Since then, in probably the single most important stride bodybuilding has taken in this country, the AAU has become the American affiliate of the IFBB. There is still factionalism, and still some displeasure with the present organizational state of things— shortly after Mike Katz's contest, Ed Jubinville, Tom Minichiello and Harold Gibson, all contest promoters, split off from the AAU/IFBB and revived an organization called the Amateur Federation of American Bodybuilders, which they describe as an "alternative to exploitation," an organization "owing allegiance to no commercial interest." But essentially, Ben Welder has accomplished what he set out in 1946 to do— he and his IFBB have taken over American bodybuilding and, by and large, American bodybuilding is the better for it.

George Butler directing a scene from the movie *Pumping Iron*

Maybe 150 people paid five dollars apiece to watch the prejudging of Mike's contest, and that night for the show he filled the 500-seat house. In 1972 he would have been lucky to have had 150 people at the show, and nobody but a few girl friends and parents would have paid five dollars to watch the prejudging. Other things were different as well. In '72 the contest would probably have been held in a YMCA gym under lights strung on a basketball rim. This year it was produced by a local theater department in a large comfortable auditorium on a professionally lit stage to piped-in music.

Mike Katz was onstage when we came in, at a microphone, explaining the prejudging to the audience. His hair was longer than in '72, he was lighter and had grown a mustache, but otherwise he hadn't changed: the pigeon chest, the slow stiff head movements, the genuineness and gravity he projects, were all still right up there at the microphone. George and I sat down and watched the prejudging, not expecting much from this small regional competition. As it happened, any one of the top five finishers at Mike Katz's contest could probably have won the Mr. America title in 1972.

The biggest change of all in bodybuilding over the past eight years is the amazing upgrading of physiques on the lower levels of competition. The Mr. Olympia competition may have remained fairly static, dominated every year by the same people, but regional competition everywhere in the country has come a long, long way. The fact is that while there may be as few great active bodybuilders now as there were in 1972, there are many more good ones. Take Len Archambault, for example, a bodybuilder George and I had first seen eight years ago in Holyoke. In 1972 Archambault was a middling competitor with skinny legs, good lats and no chest, who seemed destined to go on placing fourth in regional competitions for as long as he competed. This year, though he only took second place in Katz's small New England contest, he won his weight division at Schwarzenegger's Mr. International Competition—with a field of twenty-seven bodybuilders from ten countries—and beat out Dale Adrian, the AAU Mr. America of 1975, in doing so.

235

Sunrise, Sydney, Australia:
Arm

What the hell happened, you might wonder, to Len Archambault? Well, muscularity happened to him, as it did to hundreds of other builders between 1972 and the present. In '72, in any contest but the America, Universe or Olympia, the winner would almost always be either a brute with big smooth muscles, or a little gymnast-type with cuts but no mass. Neither of these guys would win a Mr. South Hartford contest now, because everybody else, it seems, has got muscularity—which is a combination of both size *and* clarity of the muscles. Everybody is both big *and* ripped, and anything less than that combination won't win you much. There are a number of reasons why this is so now and why it wasn't in '72, but mostly it has to do with the fact that those eight years coincided with an unprecedented national interest and education in the body, as a result of which bodybuilders are infinitely more sophisticated about training, diet, and the use of drugs now than they were in '72.

They train harder than they did then, and faster: "bombing," as Arnold taught them how to do in his mail-order courses and magazine articles, by doing a lot of repetitions with heavy weights and resting as little as possible. They have also learned since '72 that aerobic exercise, such as running and cycling, is the best way to build stamina for heavier, faster workouts, as well as being the best method for burning off stored fat and thus for polishing muscularity just before a contest. As for diet, it used to be thought that the way to eat for a contest was first a lot and then a little—to bulk up to as much as twenty or thirty percent more than what you wanted your weight to be for the contest, and then to cut back down. That is not thought anymore, now that it is known you lose as much muscle as fat that way. Bodybuilders now stay on high-protein, medium low-carbohydrate diets most of the time, keeping within five to ten percent of their contest weights, and cut back on calories just before a contest. In line with that pattern, there has also been a move away from the ingesting of four to five hundred grams of protein a day to something more like one gram per pound of body weight. The daily use of pounds of vitamin and mineral supplements is out too now, though liver-enhancing substances such as choline and lecithin are still being widely and heavily used, according to John Balik, one of the top non-professional nutrition and drug experts in bodybuilding—as are potassium and certain glandular concentrates, among them a potion of gorilla glands said to be favored by a well-known West Coast bodybuilder.

The use of steroids too has changed considerably since 1972, and that change has had as much to do as anything with the new muscularity. Oral steroids such as Dianabol and Anavar used to be employed, often in massive doses, primarily to gain weight; but those drugs, it was found, changed electrolyte balances in the body, causing it to retain water, bloating it and smoothing the muscles. Builders are now using steroids not as much to grow as to hold on to muscle during the period right before a contest when they are cutting back on calories. They are using lower dosages—say 1 cc a week spread over a number of days, as opposed to 3 or 4 cc's; and they are using injectable, slow-acting steroids such as Primobolan Acetate, a German product, or its American counterpart, Deca-Durabolin, which do not cause the body to retain water.

Great bodybuilders are still rare, because greatness in this sport and art requires the right genes—or, as Arnold Schwarzenegger has put it, the right choice of parents—in addition to everything else. But with all the better training, better diet and smarter use of drugs, there is a lot of muscularity around now; muscularity makes for good bodybuilders, ones that are fun to watch, and there are a lot of them around too, as was evident at Mike Katz's contest. The contest had two classes, under 175 pounds and over, and in each there were three or four competitors in superb shape with good posing routines: Archambault, Skip Robinson, Pat Hayes, Craig Cole, a professional wrestler named Ivan Putski, and the winner, a beautifully chiseled black bodybuilder named Ron Mangum. The prejudging was well staged, smooth and polished, and when it was over I went backstage to congratulate Mike Katz.

Calves

He was sitting at a desk in a little office, eating grapes. He is thirty-five now. In 1976, after losing to Ken Waller and Franco in the Mr. Olympia contest, Mike retired from competition, embittered over the growing use of steroids. Since then he had been teaching high school, serving as the AAU bodybuilding chairman for the State of Connecticut, producing a few shows and raising his kids. Recently he had opened up a new gym, World Gym East, and, as with most everything else in his life, Mike was proud of it. But, he said, despite all that—despite the pleasure he got from his kids and his gym and his contests—he felt incomplete without competition, and he had decided to go back to it this year. He would start with Chet Yorton's All Natural Mr. America contest in October, and then enter Arnold's Pro Mr. Universe in November. "I've got to prove something," he said. "I've got to prove that a natural bodybuilder, one who doesn't use drugs, can compete against anyone in the world . . . Also I've grown a lot—I know where my weaknesses are now and I know how to improve them. And I've got time. If you look at the top ten guys in the world, you're looking at bodybuilders between thirty-five and forty-five years old. So, I mean, I've got ten years."

He said that his training was better than ever, less rote and more instinct, and he pulled up his pants legs to show how his calves, always one of his weakest areas, were benefiting from it. "See, my whole life has been one of self-improvement. I started with less than some people, whether it's artistically, or in bodybuilding, or personality—I know I'm not perfect and I've always tried to make myself better. Going back into competition is just another way of doing that." Too, he said, he missed the limelight. The book and film versions of *Pumping Iron* had made him a sort of star, recognized in airports, spoken to on the streets. "I've missed that. It made me feel good for people to know who I am, whether that's right or wrong, and I started to see that fading, the light flickering a little, you know, since

Frank Zane

Mike Katz at his contest

I wasn't competing . . . I mean I loved being recognized. I *loved* it—the book and the movie were the greatest things that ever happened in my life."

His chest was a little down, his arms were a little up and his calves were, finally, about the same as they were in 1972. He didn't use steroids anymore, and he was eating more fish and poultry now than red meat. On the whole he was happy and satisfied, but not entirely, and so he was going back to competition—but on his own terms. "I'm not going to move to California. I'm not going to use drugs, and I'm not going to be anybody's yes-man, even to win the Mr. Olympia. I mean I'm older now and I have priorities. Competition is competition, but it's not the only thing. Even though I'm going back to win, there are other important things in my life now. You know, my family, the teaching, putting on these contests to give other guys a chance—and bodybuilding will just have to share a space with them. I just want . . . you know mostly what I want? To get back on a stage, compete again, and not embarrass myself."

I didn't see Mike at the All Natural Mr. America contest but I did see him at the Pro Mr. Universe competition on November 1st in Columbus, Ohio: he looked a little too thin, his weak points were still weak, and he didn't place; but he posed well, going out of his free routine with his crab pose and a big blown kiss to the audience, and he certainly didn't embarrass himself.

Ed Corney was in the same competition. At the show on Saturday night he posed last in the lightweight class, and Mike Katz followed him, posing first in the heavyweight class. It was like Baghdad in 1972, watching them one after another—Katz in his brown trunks, throwing out his monster side-chest and crab shots, lumbering and dramatic; Corney with his sweet, inimitable grace, gliding and plunging, opening each shot with his fingers—and the audience loved it. Ed didn't place in the contest either. He had come in too light at 169 pounds, but he looked very crisp and hard and his routine, as always, got twice the applause and stamping and screaming of anyone else's.

The next day at breakfast I asked Ed why he was, at forty-eight years old, still the best poser in bodybuilding. "I guess because it's more important to me than to a lot of other fellas," he said. "I can feel it. I can *feel* it—it's my form of communication. With me it's very personal, very emotional—it's my true self coming out, my way of telling people who I am."

Ed has been married to his second wife for four years and has two children by her, a four-year-old son and a three-year-old daughter, as well as a twenty-two-year-old daughter from his first marriage and a grandchild. He still lives in San Jose but he is out of the nightclub bouncing business, having gotten "too expert at it" and run into some trouble with the law a few years back as a result. He now makes what he calls a "struggling living" at bodybuilding; but he has been a competitive bodybuilder since 1967, and more and more, recently, he

Best in New England Body Building
Championships

240

Arnold Caesar

thinks about retiring.

"I haven't won a competition since Baghdad. Oh, I've placed, not very high, but fourths don't earn you much. Possibly I'll stay in it for one more year . . . but see I say this *every* year. I enjoy getting in shape and competing against the younger fellas. Sometimes I feel I'm handicapped because of my age, and sometimes I feel, well, I've got so much more going for me. I mean, is winning everything? Sometimes you feel it is, sometimes you feel it isn't. You know we're all human—we all want to find that pot of gold . . ."

Like Mike Katz, Ed received attention after the book and film versions of *Pumping Iron*, and also like Katz he did little to capitalize on it financially. Sometimes now, regarding his future after bodybuilding and seeing all the new money everywhere around him, he feels that maybe he missed the boat by not starting a gym or something back then when people were stopping him on the streets, and recognizing him in restaurants. But then he thinks about it, smiles that abidingly gentle smile of his that must have dangerously confused a lot of bouncers, shrugs, and says what the hell—he might not have liked the boat or the people on it anyway.

"I've got no complaints," he told me after breakfast. "Complaints don't get you anywhere but into the grave. I've taken a very liberal attitude toward life and I think that's my secret. You know ups and downs are part and parcel of the same thing and I don't get too upset over either one. My hair is a little grayer, yeah. But I feel good and I'm still good at what I do. I have some sort of fame, which is great; I use it when it's time to, other than that I don't dwell on it . . . The thing is, things move on, you know. Like here's a funny story. When my son was three months old we entered him in a beauty contest and I was the only father on the stage with the babies and mothers. His class was three months. It was a beauty contest—the best-looking baby—so they called me to present my son to the panel of judges, and I stepped forward, threw him up at arm's length where he stood up straight on the palm of my hand, holding his balance and just stood there smiling at everyone. Of course, this really scared the other ladies and the judges' panel. Then I took my hand away and he free-fell and I caught him before he hit the floor. Well he won his beauty class, got a trophy from that. Then he won the Count title—he became Count, and his trophy is as large as my Mr. America trophy. A reporter found out who I was, Mr. Universe, so he took a picture with the audience in the background, my son crawling on the floor next to his trophy, and the caption went 'Winner Crawls in Father's Footsteps.'"

The Professional Mr. Universe and Mr. International contests were produced by Arnold and by Jim Lorimer at the big auditorium in Columbus, Ohio, where they have mounted a lot of good competitions since 1975. It was a beautifully organized and produced show, if soured somewhat by the controversy over the Mr. Olympia contest, held a few weeks earlier in Australia, and by the attendant refusal of a number of top bodybuilders to compete in the Pro Mr. Universe. There were seventeen countries represented in the two competitions, and 140 people had worked part-time for a year on Lorimer's various committees to make sure that every contestant got his round-trip ticket in advance, that he had a comfortable hotel room to stay in and, if necessary, someone to translate for him, and that he was met at the airport when he arrived. There were over 500 people at the prejudging of the two contests, a packed house of 4,000 at the show that night, and $22,000 worth of prize money in the Pro Mr. Universe competition. It was a *big* show, even by 1980 standards, and it was managed deftly, with Prussian efficiency, by Arnold and Lorimer.

In 1972 there was one annual professional competition in bodybuilding, the Mr. Olympia, and its winner took home $1,000. In 1980 there were nearly a dozen professional contests with total prize money of nearly $300,000, according to Joe Weider; and this year the Mr. Olympia winner was paid $20,000 out of a $50,000 total purse. Both artistically and financially, the most significant thing to happen recently in professional bodybuilding was the establishment in 1979 of a Grand Prix circuit of professional contests. In 1980 there were five Grand Prix competitions held between February and May in Florida, Louisiana, California, Pennsylvania and New York, each paying $15,000 in prize money. The contests are invitational, and airfare, hotel expenses and a food allowance are supplied to the top ten seeds. Points are awarded along with cash prizes to each of the top ten finishers in each competition, and at the end of the circuit the overall champion receives the Joe Weider Trophy and a solid gold ring. This year's Grand Prix overall winner, edging out Casey Viator in three out of five contests for the title, was Chris Dickerson— another bodybuilder who has been around for a long time, and who is over forty years old. To their credit, the organizers of the Grand Prix circuit, Wayne DeMilia, Charles Blake and Karen Clark, have determined to experiment with staging, lighting and music for their contests, and have produced some interesting results. Each Grand Prix contest is preceded by an audio-visual slide show on the history of bodybuilding in which slides of old and new stars are synchronized by computer to appropriate period music. The contests themselves are individually choreographed, each contestant posing to music he has selected for himself and rehearsed to. And next year, Physique Productions—as DeMilia, Blake and Clark call themselves— plans to fool around a little with smoke, fog, special-effects lighting and off-platform posing as part of their continuing interest in making Grand Prix shows livelier and more artistic. "Already," says Wayne DeMilia, "compared to ours, the Mr. Olympia is a *morbid* contest."

The big amateur shows have grown and improved too, particularly the lFBB Mr. Universe contest, the World Amateur Championships. In 1972 at the Baghdad Mr. Universe contest described in the original text of this book, there were thirty-two countries represented and sixty competitors. In 1979 over 150 bodybuilders from

Ron Teufel

forty-four countries competed in the amateur Mr. Universe held in Columbus. Since 1972 first ABC and then CBS have broadcast these competitions (Ben Weider claims that the contest is seen now by 750,000,000 people in over ninety countries) and as a result they too, like the professional contests, have gotten spiffier year by year to look at.

The art has been improved then by quite a margin over its state in 1972: the bodies are better, and the presentation of them at formal shows both amateur and professional is far more sophisticated. The Mr. International/Pro Mr. Universe show that night of November 1st in Columbus was an excellent case in point. Both competitions were a mixture of old and new faces. Along with Len Archambault from Mike Katz's competition, Dale Adrian, the 1975 AAU Mr. America, Leon Brown, who won the 1972 Mr. East Coast contest described in the earlier chapters of *Pumping Iron*, and Eddie Guiliano, the old Gold's Gym court jester, were entered in the Mr. International, lats by pecs with a number of very good newcomers. In the light-heavyweight class (one of four in the competition) there were Ron Teufel, Les Galvin, who is built like a striated howitzer shell, and a blond, delighted-looking Swede, an ex-Sumo wrestler named Andreas Cahling, who won the class and later that night, with a sort of bouncy, thoughtless joy, the contest. In the heavyweight class there was Billy Arlen from Houston—a nice, well-spoken man, with marvelous proportion and balance to his physique—who won the class; and Scott Wilson, whose body, in its remarkable marriage of mass and definition, its depth and clarity of muscle and the degree of development found in obscure areas like the rear deltoids and serratus, is typical of both the new look in bodybuilding and the quality of physiques found more or less at large now in the sport.

Backstage, between the two contests that night, you could see a legislative extension of the old and new mixture: the Weider brothers again; Ricky Wayne, the nearly-great West Indian bodybuilder of a decade ago, lounging against a door and talking intelligent muscle politics; the elfin little English official, Oscar State, scurrying around with papers in his hands and a cool, appraising eye; and clumps of new-bodybuilding journalists and promoters, sponsors and officials. The full, noisy house of 4,000 people muttered and rumbled out front, gearing up for the Pro Mr. Universe, and when the officials backstage finally let it loose on them, they whistled and clapped and hollered and applauded almost continuously through the awarding of the trophies.

There were eight contestants in the lightweight class of the Pro Mr. Universe, and they were all very, very good. Mohammed Makkaway, the little Egyptian who won his division in the Amateur Mr. Universe competition in 1976 and whom I first saw in Baghdad in '72, was in nearly perfect shape, as massive for his size and as cleanly cut as a tiny Chris Dickerson. Roy Duvall from England was elegant and fine-lined. Bob Birdsong, who won his class in the '75 Universe, was another bodybuilder making a comeback, in his case from" . . . liquor, drugs, women, cars, the whole trip" via Christianity;

Robbie Robinson

Tom Platz

245

and though his wasp-waist and fabulous back were the same, the born-again grin on his face as he posed was new. Steve Davis pranced out onto the stage, looking nervous. I had talked to Davis earlier at the prejudging and he told me in his quiet, sensitive way that he had been hearing voices lately, voices imparting to him considerable psychic energy as well as the information that he was going to win that night. After he calmed down on stage he posed well, showing his sleek, well-balanced physique to advantage with calm, statuesque shots, his face full of mystical elation, and he looked good—but, the voices notwithstanding, not good enough to win. Neither did Ed Corney look good enough to win, though he looked very good; but the response to his liquid posing made the seats in the auditorium shake. The eventual winner of the class posed right before Ed. His name is Tom Platz, and he is possibly the best of the new American bodybuilders. He has yellow hair, square jaws, and possibly the most muscular legs in the history of the sport. Platz's legs make you catch your breath, and the rest of him is not far behind. Another class winner of the Amateur Mr. Universe title, he is only twenty-six, which is young for a world-class bodybuilder; with a little more chest and shoulders and a little more overall polish to his upper body, he is going to be hard for anybody to beat for a long time.

Mike Katz posed first in the heavyweight class, without embarrassing himself. He was followed by Albert Beckles, who won the Mr. Universe title way hack in 1971. Beckles is a West Indian who now lives in England. He has been around for a long time, but his arms and his back seem to get younger and better every year. And following Beckles were two relative newcomers, Greg DeFerro, and a German postal employee, another Mr. Universe class winner, named Jusup Wilcosz. DeFerro, who looks a little like Sylvester Stallone and was nicknamed Rocky by the chanting crowd, was deep, thick, and cut. He looked wonderful; but Wilcosz looked better. Wilcosz trained for this contest for most of a year under Arnold Schwarzenegger's supervision, and it showed. He had size, shape, clarity and proportion of muscle, and he also had an Arnold-like finish to his body—an intricate and polished coming together of interrelated parts, the look of which is as satisfying, and in the same way satisfying, to the eye as the sound of a closing Mercedes door is to the ear. Wilcosz is bearded and grizzled-looking; he did not pose with much joy or flair, but he was the best new bodybuilder I saw work in 1980. He is the state of the new art and, though it was difficult to identify with his routine, the crowd knew that. During the pose-off between the top three men in both classes and after it—after Makkaway was given his sixth-place trophy, and DeFerro his fifth, Beckles his fourth, Birdsong his third, and Platz his second—the audience stayed with Wilcosz, and met his overall title with pandemonium.

Of the six top finishers in the 1980 Pro Mr. Universe contest three were relative newcomers, and three were competing eight years ago in 1972. It was a fitting end to the competition, given how intimately

Boyer Coe

Tom Platz

and uniquely bodybuilding lives with its past, with its living ghosts. But the real end to the evening was not that. The real end was more ghostly still: the whole audience chanting for Arnold, drowning out his thanking it for coming, most of the people in it thunderously wanting him—bodybuilding's greatest and most stirring ghost, its most arrogant and puckish ghost—to strip off his clothes and pose; others wanting his head.

They wanted those different things, members of the two factions in the audience of the Pro Mr. Universe show, for the same reason: because a few weeks before in the Sydney, Australia, Opera House Arnold had won his seventh Mr. Olympia title.

It was not a simple victory. In fact it caused, at the time and for months afterwards, an incredible uproar, reminiscent of the old chaos-days of bodybuilding. It caused a still-reverberating shakeup in international judging procedures, a near fistfight between Arnold and Mike Mentzer, and the threatened retirement of some of bodybuilding's top competitors, among them Mentzer, Boyer Coe and Frank Zane—each of whom thought he should have won the Olympia title himself and was positive that Arnold should not have. And most disturbingly, maybe, it caused Arnold, who is bodybuilding for most of the world, to be booed by a crowd, there in Sydney, for the first time in his career.

George Butler was in Sydney; I was not. But I have seen the pictures and talked to a lot of people about it, and I have a pretty good idea of how things went. Early on, the competition seemed to be shaping up to be one of the best in bodybuilding history. Frank Zane, the defending champion, Mike Mentzer, Boyer Coe, Chris Dickerson, and Dennis Tinnerino were all in top shape. Tinnerino claimed to be in the best shape of his life. Coe came in for the first time in his career weighing more than 200 pounds, and all of his muscle was very close to the skin. Dickerson, hot off his string of wins on the Grand Prix, was polished and tighter than ever; and Frank Zane, despite an injury suffered during training, could not have been more defined, Mike Mentzer figured that he had the best chance of all: he had scored a perfect 300 at this contest the year before; he had trained brutally hard for nearly six months for this year's contest, and had added ten pounds of cut muscle. There was no way, Mentzer thought, he could lose this year. Yet he did, as did the others—and none of them liked it.

When he learned he had won second place, Chris Dickerson said "Oh, no!" and disappeared into the Australian night. Frank Zane smashed his third-place trophy on the asphalt of the Opera House parking lot. Boyer Coe, who took fourth place, reportedly asked out loud if there was no justice, and then sent chairs flying into walls. And Mike Mentzer was quoted as saying about his placing fifth: "I'll tell you, somebody out there wanted me crushed out completely. Well that's it for me. That's the last time I'm going through that kind of training for that kind of shit decision . . . Bodybuilding just lost what could have been its best spokesman."

Straining and stretching

Mike Mentzer and Arnold
in Sydney, Australia

Why all the temper and sour grapes, you might wonder? They did, after all, lose to Arnold, and there is nothing unusual about that. Well for one thing, because very few people who were there, other than the judges and Franco Columbu and Arnold himself, thought Arnold was in good enough shape to win. Most of the fifteen competitors in the contest thought he shouldn't have won; the booers in the Opera House audience thought he shouldn't have won; and for another thing, Coe and Zane and Mentzer and Tinnerino and others felt not only unfairly beaten, but used and had by Arnold; his victory, they felt, denigrated them and cheapened the sport.

That line of feeling runs something like this: here was Arnold, retired now for five years, rich and famous and *out* of competitive bodybuilding, and all of a sudden for no good reason he decides to get back into it, only he doesn't tell anyone; he trains for only *seven weeks,* which is an afternoon compared to what most of the others put in, and tells anyone who asks that he is training for a part in a movie he is about to make, and then he comes over to Sydney where he is supposed to do color commentary on the contest for CBS but instead, once he is there, once they're all there and it's too late for anyone to back out, he announces that he thinks he might as well compete—I mean he's already won the title six times and he sure as hell doesn't need the money or the fame, but . . . as long as he's here—so he hops into a contest full of guys who would kill to win it just once, five of the seven judges of which are good friends of his . . . and he *wins* the thing. At the end of that line of feeling is this question: what does all that say about how Arnold *feels* about us, the competitors who follow and in some cases emulate him, and about bodybuilding itself, the thing we still do with all four feet? It was that question really, and the insult that seemed to be the only answer to it, that caused all the furor over Sydney. It is a good question, but it misses the point.

The fact is that Arnold *does* think of bodybuilding as his personal province, into which he can step back as sovereign whenever he wants, and he *doesn't* think much of the other competitors in Sydney. He sees them as technicians, vying and squabbling among themselves for empty dominance over an era in bodybuilding that is temporarily without giants.

"If Franco and Sergio Oliva and Lou Ferrigno and Dave Draper and I would suddenly all go back into competition now," he says, "we would still rule everything. There are eras of certain people that come up that are great, and in between everything is just technical. It happens in politics—if you look at it today there are no Churchills around, nobody to really move people and make them believe in one thing, and therefore politics is just technical now. It's the same in bodybuilding—there are no giants around, and it's become a technical sport, with everybody talking about Chris Dickerson, and 'did you see Frank Zane's lower left abdominal?'—that sort of thing."

It is also a fact that he enjoyed beating the technicians—a couple of whom had been guilty of sniping at his training principles—and that

1980 Mr. Olympia Contest,
Sydney, Australia

Arnold with Joe Gold

anticipation of that enjoyment was a part of his decision to compete. "I wanted to have a good time with the whole thing. To go there, see them all be surprised, see them all freak out and have diarrhea, you know? And be confused and be upset about it, and have a career that they had planned for themselves go down the tube in two seconds. And I accomplished that. People are retiring now. Boyer Coe wants to retire, Mike Mentzer wants to retire, everybody wants to retire now because of this event. The only thing that means is that now I have to expand my next book—I have to add on a chapter on how to make your competition retire." But it was not the whole decision, or even the biggest part of it.

The thing that confused and angered so many people about Arnold's return to competition was that they couldn't figure it, couldn't locate it in any logic. He had everything to lose and only twenty thousand dollars, which he didn't need, to win. So why? A lot of theories were ventured—that he was doing it to perk up his movie career, or to help sell his books, or because someone had implied he couldn't win again, or because he missed the limelight—but none of those theories really seemed sufficient. It seemed, finally, to a lot of people, a kind of *crazy* thing to do, as crazy as Muhammad Ali's comeback fight against Larry Holmes, which was broadcast in Sydney the day before the Mr. Olympia contest. But Arnold's return wasn't crazy, only odd—and only odd against the gladhanding, anxiously cooperative, buck-turning backdrop of bodybuilding in 1980.

Like Muhammad Ali, Arnold doesn't play anybody's game but his own, and also like Ali, he is a brilliant hunch-player. He operates on every level of his personality without needing reasons. For better or worse, he returned to competition because he happened to be training anyway for a part in a movie and he felt like it—because some unquestioned impulse in his guts told him to.

After having studied hundreds of pictures of the contest, it looks to me like he should have won. He himself acknowledges that he had only eighty to ninety percent of his overall shape of 1975, and that his legs were weak; but his arms and back and chest were there, and in the pictures he looks, even at eighty to ninety percent, to have more symmetry and flow to his body than anyone else. I wasn't there, and no matter how many pictures 1 look at 1 won't ever really know how the physiques compared. But I do know why Arnold won. He won because he is a great competitor; exactly as he says he is, Arnold is a giant. He won because of that, and he should have. The point missed by the competitors who felt cheapened and belittled and insulted by Arnold's victory is this: it is giants, and only giants, who carry bodybuilding forward. And every victory for them is a victory for the art and sport.

Leg curls

Jusup Wilcosz training with Arnold

Franco Columbu is another giant, albeit a short one. Eight years ago when I first started to write on bodybuilding, he and Arnold were the top of the heap, and they still are. Franco is bemused by what Arnold

did in Sydney. He thinks he just might do the same thing next year when the Mr. Olympia contest will be held in Columbus. I went to see him recently in Los Angeles to talk to him about that and other things.

He was wearing a blue T-shirt that said "Vitalis," the product he is paid an annual salary to advertise on TV and was pacing around the big empty new offices on Westwood Boulevard into which the following day he was moving his profitable chiropractic and mail-order businesses. Parked outside in the lot was his red Alfa Romeo.

Franco prefers the word superstar to giant. Practically everybody now, he says, is a star in bodybuilding—all those guys with 3 percent bodyfat who win the Mr. America and Mr. Universe contests and who all look alike. But there have only been, ever, a few superstars. Namely, said Franco, "John Grimek, Steve Reeves, Reg Park, Sergio Oliva, Arnold and Franco." And those few have prerogatives: "Arnold won the Olympia this year just to show them he can do it. And I'm going to do it next year, maybe, because we want to show them that if we want, we keep the Olympia forever . . . I would like everybody to know that we might come back and win it anytime."

Franco came over to America at the end of 1969 with a thousand dollars in cash and very little English. Now eleven years later, he is a TV personality on talk shows as well as in commercials, a bodybuilding superstar, and a wealthy man. He accomplished all that in the same way Arnold did—by refusing to take it easy on himself, and by extending himself variously to meet what both of them perceived to be the endless possibilities in this country. "Here in America the opportunities are unlimited. But you have to do it yourself. In other words, over here people say, look, you want it? Get it. That's why me and Arnold are successful here. It's because when we came everybody was lying on the beach doing nothing. There were a hundred bodybuilders lying out there doing nothing. So I said to Arnold what the hell are we doing here, why don't we go do something? And Arnold said sure, let's get out of here. So we go get jobs laying brick, and we train hard and win contests, then we start writing books and making movies. Arnold went to business administration school and I went to chiropractor college, and six years later I've got a degree and I go back out to the beach and those same guys are still lying there. I say 'Huh! What are you waiting for, Christmas?'"

Franco is still extending, and loving every minute of it. After he wins the Olympia again, he'd like to do certain movies. "Like, actually I would like to do one very nice love movie, and the next one should be a very brutal one, totally the opposite." And he wouldn't mind serving in politics as a sort of adviser, "to look around in the cities and see all the things wrong and report back to the city and say I would like to see things done this way, and do this kind of changes."

And he is going back to college again this summer, to get a Ph.D. in nutrition and prepare himself for the ultimate superstar's extension: "I want to get so involved in nutrition and know so much about the body that I can live much longer than normal. I think there's a

1980 Mr. Olympia Contest

256

Arnold with Maria Shriver

possibility that we can live between a hundred twenty and a hundred fifty years, and that's what I want to do."

Franco took me back to his house later to watch tapes of his Vitalis commercials which, he says, have boosted the company's sales to their highest point in fifty years. He is wonderful in them—sly, disarming, pungent—and he watches them with pleasure and funny stories about their production. He looks exactly the same as he did in 1972, both on screen and in person: the joy and cuteness, the irrepressibility, haven't worn off or even down in his face. Watching him sell the hell out of hair oil on television, I asked him if he and Arnold were still close.

"Me and Arnold, we are very busy doing so many things, we travel in different directions. But he's my best friend and I'm his best friend. When he needs help I help him, and when I need help he helps me. And when we get together, we are the same. There's nothing changed. We get together, we go to the same places—we play like two kids, we play very hard. We go and play bowling, we play chess and we don't even know how to play chess. Then we still drive the cars. We go up to the mountains and see how fast the cars go. You know? One time we almost fell over the hill. And that is important, the mind needs that."

"The paump by Vitalis," adds the television Franco, *"holds* and *holds* and *holds* some more . . . the *paump*—by Vitalis."

Franco's best friend lives in a $700,000 house on a quiet, expensive, palm-lined street in Santa Monica. Outside the house in the driveway are a Mercedes and a doozied-up Jeep Cherokee. Inside is a portrait of Arnold by Jamie Wyeth, a photograph of him with Ted Kennedy, another with Jimmy Carter. The furniture, the paintings, the rugs, the books, everything in the house, reflects Arnold's uncanny ability to grow in a variety of ways at once and to assimilate quality as quickly and efficiently as he does protein. I went by to see him at this new house a few days after I saw Franco. It was a perfect Southern California afternoon, and we sat outside by his black-bottomed swimming pool, his guest house and hot-tub Jacuzzi behind us. Over a month had gone by since Sydney, and Arnold was leaving shortly for Spain to play Conan the Barbarian, in a $15,000,000 film of that name. He was expansive and relaxed, and we talked all afternoon. When I lit a cigar he went and got a big Cuban number and lit up too; one of his two secretaries came by to check on a problem with the security alarm system. Late that afternoon, taking a Jacuzzi before we went to dinner, he looked around his darkening property and said, "I love this new house. I like to think about myself like a snake—I rest up here, like under a rock, save myself, grow strong, and then when I'm ready I jump out and strike, make my move."

Hoarding himself didn't occur to Arnold in 1972. I asked him what had changed in his life to make it necessary now.

"Well, first of all my life is much more hectic now than it was when we first met. Back then all I had to be concerned with was to train, to go to school, and to take care of my mail-order business. Now, of course, there are so many other things. I'm always working on a book for instance. I'm always preparing for some film, taking sword-fighting lessons, horseback riding lessons, voice lessons to get rid of some of the bad pronunciations, and all those things. The office now has so many responsibilities—I manage my money and real estate, and produce shows, you know, with raising money and organizing and doing advertising and all those things. Which means I have to get up at 6:30 in the morning, I have to do my running then and go to the gym, so by 9 o'clock I have my breakfast behind me and all my training is done. In the evening I maybe take dance lessons and lessons on how to lift a woman, or do the sword fighting for Conan and so on. And during the day I do all the business—answering mail, phone calls for an hour or two in the morning, and then it is working on the book, picking photos for the book, or setting up seminars, or doing exhibitions in prisons. So now the whole day is occupied. The year is occupied now with ten different things, where there were only three things before. I feel now that I'm a combination of a business man, actor, producer of bodybuilding shows, and also, like this year, I was a competitor. So that's quite a bit going on . . . " He looked out over the roof line of his house. Like Franco's, his face hasn't changed in eight years. His hard, honest eyes are as avid as they were in '72; his grin is as mischievous and open and quick. "I enjoy it, though. I feel that if I don't do something all the time I'm wasting my life. I'm the most comfortable when I'm busy and when I do things and accomplish things. The point is to go somewhere, and that has been my life, working toward something and keeping things up."

I asked him if he missed his old anonymity, and the old gaiety and carelessness that anonymity afforded him. "Yeah, I miss it. I mean you wish you could have two lives. Before 1975, when I wanted to light up a joint at a party I lit it up, because I didn't have national recognition. Now I can't do that anymore. I haven't had a joint in my hand since 1975. I haven't done anything to harm my career since 1975. But the reason why that doesn't annoy me is that I've always had to give things up, all my life, to achieve what I wanted."

At thirty-four years old, he has already achieved much of what he set out from Graz, Austria, twelve years ago to achieve. He wanted to be the world's best bodybuilder, and he is. He wanted to be famous, and he is. He wanted to be rich, and he is that too—by his own definition a millionaire who no longer has to think about money. Either directly or indirectly, he achieved all those things through bodybuilding, at which he worked as hard as anyone has ever worked at anything. That work combined with his splendid genes to make him a giant in bodybuilding. And as he proved in Sydney, he's still a giant there, though now a largely disaffected one. He believes that the sport and art of bodybuilding are overpopulated now with midget

Robbie Robinson and Ed Corney

259

Arnold with Charles Gaines, Philadelphia, 1980

technicians and hustlers, in it only to make a buck instead of to locate the joy and pride he found there and to let the bucks take care of themselves. The goals he is always setting for himself lie outside of bodybuilding now. He is now, finally, after Sydney, bored and disillusioned with bodybuilding, and ready to go be a giant elsewhere.

He thinks he might someday get into politics. Eventually he wants a sturdy and fun-loving wife, children, a big home in the American West with high ceilings and simple rugged furniture, and land. In the meantime, he wants to be a giant in films.

"I think I could be and will be a heroic character. I would like to do heroic films. I'd like to be like Clint Eastwood, someone who takes what they have and makes something out of it, not trying to change . . . I think I can go all the way in that, and eventually get into producing, because I like the business end of the things I do as much as just being always the talent."

Arnold also wants to go on being an effective inspiration and model to as many people as possible; he wants to work with prisoners and retarded children; he wants to learn to ski better and play better tennis, to act better and read better books. Though he didn't mention it, he may well want real estate on the moon. Giants have big appetites. "You never get where everything is done. You have always this new thing in front of you, so you then work toward that, so it's an everlasting hunger for new things, for achieving something else."

More than anything else, Arnold says, he wants to stay hungry, and it is that word more than any other that still describes him. Back in 1968 he came to this country and picked up the art and the sport of bodybuilding where the last giant had left them. Almost single-handedly, he carried them a long way to the present. Now he has put them down again and gone on to other things. It remains to be seen who will pick them up next, and in what direction they will be carried.

Afterword

One evening in the summer of 1960, when I was about sixteen, I saw something that, even though I was not yet a photographer, amazed me with its visual power. The memory of what I saw that night remains as clear and as much a part of what intrigues me about bodybuilding as the most recent images of Arnold Schwarzenegger competing at the Sydney Opera House twenty years later.

It all took place in a church in Savanna-la-,Mar, Jamaica, where I lived at the time. I was sitting in the church's mahogany balcony because a friend, Dr. Herbert Eldemire, was running for a seat in the Jamaican legislature. Only in Jamaica could one run for political office in the pulpit of an eighteenth-century church, overlooked by colonial memorials and backed by a "rock steady" band with the smell of frangipani blossoms heavy in the air.

Herbie rose to the occasion and delivered a colorful, anti-colonial speech. He was an ex-boxing champion of the Empire and fond of delivering blows to the English chin. As he neared the end, he began waving a bulletwood cudgel over his head. "Vote for me," he roared, "and I will lead the western parishes of Cornwall out of the British Empire as Moses led the children of Israel from Egypt!"

In 1960 independence was in the air and it was a suitable climax to a rowdy evening. As everyone got up to leave, however, Herbie thumped the floor with his cudgel: "Hold it brothers," he commanded. "We still have added entertainment. My friend and loyal Jamaica Labour Party supporter, Mr. Lloyd George Young, has brought with him from Montego Bay a monument to the strength of our future nation."

The rock steady band started a version of "*God Save the Queen*" as polite applause greeted a distinguished-looking man in a white suit.

"Please fix the light, Phonso,"said Mr. Young, while he took Herbie's place in the pulpit. A broad-shouldered electrician scaled the church wall to the rafter above the altar and began struggling with a spotlight. In a moment the church was plunged into darkness.

"P.N.P. sabotage!" yelled a voice, referring to the rival political party.

"No, man. Is me. Fuse blow," shouted Phonso from high over the confusion. '

The parson began handing out candles and bottled flares. "Let there be light," he said as Phonso dropped from the air. '

The room Was illuminated and Lloyd George, after waiting for order, leaned forward over the parish's open bible. "I am proud to present," he said, "the runner-up in the Mr. Universe contest held last year in the Albert Hall, London." He looked solemnly at the east door of the church. "Samson, are you ready?"

A tall undressed man sprang from this threshold (leaving a track of coconut-oil footprints in the aisle) loped to the altar, and began displaying an incredible body to the congregation.

That was my introduction to bodybuilding. I'm not sure a pillar of fire or a live appearance by the angel Gabriel could have outdone the splendor of the demonstration. The audience, quieter now and in fine emotional step with the proceedings, began murmuring approval.

Samson exhibited his chest, abdomen, and a lot of other muscles I'd never seen before. "All right," said Lloyd George."Let's have a back pose." Phonso, flexing his own massive arms to the delight of everyone, held two kerosene flares up to the ebony back that was pivoting into focus. It revealed an adzed shield of muscle, hovering like a specter in front of the altar cloths. As Samson flexed, the church broke into the loudest applause of the evening.

Ten years after this memorable vision, I met Charles Gaines in New Hampshire, where we both live. Charles asked me to take the photographs for a magazine article about a small bodybuilding contest in Holyoke, Massachusetts. I took the assignment because I remembered that night in Jamaica. That assignment led, through some equally exotic scenery, to this book—which is what, in the end, has made it all so worthwhile.

I'm grateful to Charles for this and for his company along the way. Also to Dan Green for being the lonely editor who gambled on us when no one else would, and to Marty Moskof, the skillful designer of this book.

Everyone who has worked with us on this book, the movie and the other enterprises along the way joins us in thanking the competitors and organizers of the IFBB for their wholehearted participation and good will from the beginning.

George Butler
Holderness, N.H.
1 August 1981

All photographs in this book (with the exception of the historical material) were taken with a Leica M4 camera with a Leitz Summilux 1.4/35mm lens. Throughout I used Kodak Tri-X film with available light only.

Authors Charles Gaines and George Butler with Arnold Schwarzenegger

Pumping Iron
is also available as an e-book
for Kindle, Amazon Fire, iPad, Nook, and Android e-readers.
Visit creatorspublishing.com to learn more.

∘ ∘ ∘

CREATORS PUBLISHING

We find compelling storytellers and
help them craft their narrative,
distributing their novels and collections
worldwide.

∘ ∘ ∘

Made in the USA
Monee, IL
29 August 2024

64775200R00149